3 5 7 9 10 8 6 4

Vintage
20 Vauxhall Bridge Road,
London SW1V 2SA

Vintage Classics is part of the Penguin Random House
group of companies whose addresses can be found at
global.penguinrandomhouse.com

Penguin
Random House
UK

First published in Great Britain by Chatto & Windus in 1999
This short edition published by Vintage in 2017

penguin.co.uk/vintage

A CIP catalogue record for this book is available from the British Library

ISBN 9781784872762

Typeset in 9.5/14.5 pt FreightText Pro
by Jouve (UK), Milton Keynes
Printed and bound by Clays Ltd, ELCOGRAF S.P.A.

Penguin Random House is committed to a sustainable future for
our business, our readers and our planet. This book is made from
Forest Stewardship Council® certified paper.

MIX
Paper from
responsible sources
FSC® C018179

Swimming

ROGER DEAKIN

VINTAGE MINIS

Contents

1

The Moat

THE WARM RAIN tumbled from the gutter in one of those midsummer downpours as I hastened across the lawn behind my house in Suffolk and took shelter in the moat. Breaststroking up and down the thirty yards of clear, green water, I nosed along, eyes just at water level. The frog's-eye view of rain on the moat was magnificent. Rain calms water, it freshens it, sinks all the floating pollen, dead bumblebees and other flotsam. Each raindrop exploded in a momentary, bouncing fountain that turned into a bubble and burst. The best moments were when the storm intensified, drowning birdsong, and a haze rose off the water as though the moat itself were rising to meet the lowering sky. Then the rain eased and the reflected heavens were full of tiny dancers: water sprites springing up on tiptoe like bright pins over the surface. It was raining water sprites.

It was at the height of this drenching in the summer of

1996 that the notion of a long swim through Britain began to form itself. I wanted to follow the rain on its meanderings about our land to rejoin the sea, to break out of the frustration of a lifetime doing lengths, of endlessly turning back on myself like a tiger pacing its cage. I began to dream of secret swimming holes and a journey of discovery through what William Morris, in the title to one of his romances, called *The Water of the Wondrous Isles*. My inspiration was John Cheever's classic short story 'The Swimmer', in which the hero, Ned Merrill, decides to swim the eight miles home from a party on Long Island via a series of his neighbours' swimming pools. One sentence in the story stood out and worked on my imagination: 'He seemed to see, with a cartographer's eye, that string of swimming pools, that quasi-subterranean stream that curved across the county.'

I was living by myself, feeling sad at the end of a long love, and, as a freelance film-maker and writer, more or less free to commit myself to a journey if I wanted to. My son, Rufus, was also on an adventure Down Under, working in restaurants and surfing in Byron Bay, and I missed him. At least I could join him in spirit in the water. Like the endless cycle of the rain, I would begin and end the journey in my moat, setting out in spring and swimming through the year. I would keep a log of impressions and events as I went.

My earliest memory of serious swimming is of being woken very early on holiday mornings with my grandparents in Kenilworth by a sudden rain of pebbles at my bedroom window aimed by my Uncle Laddie, who was a local swimming champion and had his own key to the outdoor pool. My cousins and I were reared on mythic tales of his exploits – in races, on high boards, or swimming far out to sea – so it felt an honour to swim with him. Long before the lifeguards arrived, we would unlock the wooden gate and set the straight, black, refracted lines on the bottom of the green pool snaking and shimmying. It was usually icy, but the magic of being first in is what I remember. 'We had the place to ourselves,' we would say with satisfaction afterwards over breakfast. Our communion with the water was all the more delightful for being free of charge. It was my first taste of unofficial swimming.

Years later, driven mad by the heat one sultry summer night, a party of us clambered over the low fence of the old open-air pool at Diss in Norfolk. We joined other silent, informal swimmers who had somehow stolen in, hurdling the dormant turnstiles, and now loomed past us in the water only to disappear again into the darkness like characters from *Under Milk Wood*. Such indelible swims are like dreams, and have the same profound effect on the mind and spirit. In the night sea at Walberswick I have seen bodies fiery with phosphorescent plankton striking through the neon waves like dragons.

The more I thought about it, the more obsessed I became with the idea of a swimming journey. I started to dream ever more exclusively of water. Swimming and dreaming were becoming indistinguishable. I grew convinced that following water, flowing with it, would be a way of getting under the skin of things, of learning something new. I might learn about myself, too. In water, all possibilities seemed infinitely extended. Free of the tyranny of gravity and the weight of the atmosphere, I found myself in the wide-eyed condition described by the Australian poet Les Murray when he said: 'I am only interested in everything.' The enterprise began to feel like some medieval quest. When Merlin turns the future King Arthur into a fish as part of his education in *The Sword in the Stone*, T. H. White says, 'He could do what men always wanted to do, that is, fly. There is practically no difference between flying in the water and flying in the air . . . It was like the dreams people have.'

When you swim, you feel your body for what it mostly is – water – and it begins to move with the water around it. No wonder we feel such sympathy for beached whales; we are beached at birth ourselves. To swim is to experience how it was before you were born. Once in the water, you are immersed in an intensely private world as you were in the womb. These amniotic waters are both utterly safe and yet terrifying, for at birth anything could go wrong, and you are assailed by all kinds of unknown forces over which you have no control. This may account for the anxieties every swimmer experiences from time to time in deep water. A swallow dive off the high board into the void is an image that brings together all the contradictions of birth. The swimmer experiences the terror and the bliss of being born.

So swimming is a rite of passage, a crossing of boundaries: the line of the shore, the bank of the river, the edge of the pool, the surface itself. When you enter the water, something like metamorphosis happens. Leaving behind the land, you go through the looking-glass surface and enter a new world, in which survival, not ambition or desire, is the dominant aim. The lifeguards at the pool or the beach remind you of the thin line between waving and drowning. You see and experience things when you're swimming in a way that is completely different from any other. You are *in* nature, part and parcel of it, in a far more complete and intense way than on dry land, and your sense of the present is overwhelming. In wild water you are on equal terms with the animal world around you: in every sense, on the same level. As a swimmer, I can go right up to a frog in the water and it will show more curiosity than fear. The damselflies and dragonflies that crowd the surface of the moat pointedly ignore me, just taking off for a moment to allow me to go by, then landing again in my wake.

Natural water has always held the magical power to cure. Somehow or other, it transmits its own self-regenerating powers to the swimmer. I can dive in with a long face and what feels like a terminal case of depression, and come out a whistling idiot. There is a feeling of absolute freedom and wildness that comes with the sheer liberation of nakedness

I can dive in with a long face and what feels like a terminal case of depression, and come out a whistling idiot as well as weightlessness in natural water, and it leads to a deep bond with the bathing-place.

Most of us live in a world where more and more places and things are signposted, labelled, and officially 'interpreted'. There is something about all this that is turning the reality of things into virtual reality. It is the reason why walking, cycling and swimming will always be subversive activities. They allow us to regain a sense of what is old and wild in these islands, by getting off the beaten track and breaking free of the official version of things. A swimming journey would give me access to that part of our world which, like darkness, mist, woods or high mountains, still retains most mystery. It would afford me a different perspective on the rest of landlocked humanity.

My moat, where the journey first suggested itself, and really began, is fed by a vigorous spring eleven feet down, and purified by an entirely natural filtration system far superior to even the most advanced of swimming-pool technology. It is sustained by the plant and animal life you will find in any unpolluted fresh-water pond left to its own devices and given plenty of sunlight. There seems to have been a period, from the later Middle Ages until the seventeenth century, when moats became as fashionable in Suffolk as private pools are today. There are over thirty of them within a four-mile radius of the church in the nearby village of Cotton. Moats are now considered by historians like Oliver Rackham to have functioned as much as status symbols as anything else for the yeoman farmers who dug them. Mine was probably excavated when the house was built in the sixteenth century, and runs along the front and back of the house but not the sides. It had no defensive function except as a stock barrier. It would have yielded useful clay for building and formed a substantial reservoir, but it was certainly never intended for swimming. Its banks plunge straight down and it has no shallow end. At one end, where you climb in or out by a submerged wooden cart-ladder I have staked to the bank, a big willow presides, its pale fibrous roots waving in the water like sea anemones.

The moat is where I have bathed for years, swimming breaststroke for preference. I am no champion, just a competent swimmer with a fair amount of stamina. Part of my intention in setting out on the journey was not to perform any spectacular feats, but to try and learn something of the mystery D. H. Lawrence noticed in his poem 'The Third Thing':

> Water is H_2O, hydrogen two parts, oxygen one,
> But there is also a third thing, that makes it water
> And nobody knows what that is.

Cheever describes being in the water, for Ned Merrill, as 'less a pleasure, it seemed, than the resumption of a natural condition'. My intention was to revert to a similarly feral state. For the best part of a year, the water would become my natural habitat. Otters sometimes set off across country in search of new territory, fresh water, covering as much as twelve miles in a night. I suppose there is part of all of us that envies the otter, the dolphin and the whale, our mammal cousins who are so much better adapted to water than we are, and seem to get so much more enjoyment from life than we do. If I could learn even a fraction of whatever they know, the journey would be richly repaid.

Packing, the night before I left, I felt something of the same apprehension and exhilaration as I imagine the otter might feel about going off into the blue. But, as with Ned Merrill in 'The Swimmer', my impulse to set off was simple enough at heart: 'The day was beautiful and it seemed to him that a long swim might enlarge and celebrate its beauty.'

2

I-Spy at the Seaside

Scilly Isles, 23 April

ST MARY'S ROAD AND TRESCO Flats could easily be somewhere in the East End of London, but they are the names of some of the treacherous waters that have wrecked so many ships on the islands and rocks of the Scillies. I had sailed over from Penzance on the *Scillonian* to St Mary's harbour, and was now bound for the quiet island of Bryher in an open boat with an engine like a rolling kettledrum. We chugged through the calm water of Appletree Bay in the spring sunshine, past the islands of Samson and Tresco, to land at a makeshift planked jetty known as 'Anneka's Quay' after Anneka Rice, who built it (with a little help from the Parachute Regiment) for one of those television programmes in which she performed the impossible before breakfast. Half a dozen of us disembarked along the sandy boardwalk on to the beach path, where I met the postmistress with her red bicycle waiting to hand over the mail. She directed me to a B&B, and in less than twenty minutes I had a room overlooking the bay and was on my way for a swim.

Having crossed the island in a quarter of an hour's walk, I followed a rim of doughnut rocks to the white sands of Great Popplestones Bay. Apart from a solitary sun-worshipper out of sight at the far end of the bay, I was alone. It was still April, and the swimming season could hardly be said to have begun; hence my migration to the reputedly balmy climate of these islands, 'bathed in the warm Gulf Stream', as they put it in the brochure. So far, so good. This was my first sea swim, so I thought I had better grasp the nettle of a skin baptism. I stripped off and ran naked into the water, screaming inwardly with the sudden agony of it. It was scaldingly cold, and the icy water kept on tearing pain through me until I got moving and swam a few frantic strokes as children do on their first visit to the deep end, then scrambled out breathless with cold; a mad moment of masochism. So much for the fabled caress of the gentle Gulf Stream. I climbed straight into my wetsuit and swam comfortably out again into the amazing clear water in a flat calm, crossed the little bay, marvelling at the brightness of everything, and swam back again. The sand was white and fine, and shone up through the water. Small dead crabs floated amongst the thin line of shredded bladderwrack and tiny shells oscillating up the beach. The silence was disturbed only by nature's bagpipes, the incessant gulls. I climbed out onto rocks that glinted gold with quartz and mica, stripped off the wetsuit, and lay down to dry in the sun. Spread out next to me, it looked like another sunbather.

The black rubber Bibendum travelled about with me like my shadow. I knew from the outset that I would have to confront the Wetsuit Question and concede that if I were to swim in all seasons and every variety of open water, I would need to wear one from time to time. So I had myself measured for a tailor-made suit by two friends one night in their kitchen in Suffolk. I stood in my swimming trunks before the fire after dinner while they measured me with a cloth tape from the sewing drawer. The wetsuit couturier had sent a list of the required measurements that could hardly have been more thorough had I been going into space: 'base of throat to top of leg', 'neck to shoulder edge', 'centre back to base of neck', and so on, down to the ankle circumference. When we had finished, someone discovered that the tape had shrunk an inch-and-a-quarter, so we had to re-calculate everything. But the suit fitted like a banana skin when it arrived.

The problem about wearing a wetsuit is sensory deprivation; it is a species of whole-body condom. Of course, there are people who like rubber. They enjoy the feel of it; they may even find it aesthetically pleasing. But there is no getting away from the fact that a wetsuit is an anaesthetic to prevent you experiencing the full force of your physical encounter with cold water, and in that sense it is against nature and something of a killjoy. On the other hand, I tell myself each time I struggle into the rubber, not a drop of water ever actually reaches the skin of the otter. Its outer fur traps air in an insulating layer very like a wetsuit, and the inner fur is so fine and tight together that the water never penetrates it. So if otters are allowed what amounts to a drysuit, I reckoned I could permit myself the occasional, judicious use of the wetsuit to bolster my chances of survival. It can make a long swim in cold water bearable, even comfortable, but it cannot approach the sensuality of swimming in your own skin.

At a triathlon meeting nearly everyone wears a wetsuit, and I always find the best place to witness these events is at the point where the contestants come out of the water and hurry comically towards their bikes, peeling themselves out of wet rubber as they go. It is easy to pull a muscle in the Houdini contortions sometimes necessary to escape from your suit. But some of the most useful equipment for the wild swimmer can be a pair of wetsuit boots and gloves. It is your hands and feet that will drive you out of the water before anything else.

More or less alone on the wild side of this innocent island, I felt myself slipping fast into a 'Coral Island' state of mind. There was exploring to be done. I set off past the Great Pool, a shallow fresh-water tarn outside the modest Hell Bay Hotel, the only hotel on the island, climbed Gweal Hill and found a ruined Bronze-age chambered tomb, then aimed for the shore at Stinking Porth. A pigtailed islander was repairing a low-slung cottage by the bay, and the last washing line in England was proudly flying the family underwear in the breeze. I walked along the top of the shoreline on well-sprung sea pinks. Banks of rocks and earth protected the island along this Atlantic coast, planted by the islanders with agapanthus. Its tough, adventurous roots bind the earth and rocks together and when it flowers in summer it must create a magnificent pale blue hedge along the sea. It was the first of many plants I encountered growing wild on Bryher that I was used to seeing inside conservatories. I snapped, crackled and popped along the line of dried bladderwrack that probably gave Stinking Porth its name, humming to myself and getting lost in a pleasant daze of walking-blues rhythm. I was stopped in my tracks by a dead porpoise at my feet, tangled in seaweed and oil, baring the hundreds of little saw-teeth serrating its jaw as it began to decompose; the petite, elegant tail curled by the sun as though flipping out of its bonds of black kelp. The greatest excitement of living on islands like these must be the sheer variety and constant surprise of what gets washed up on your local beach or rocks. For one woman, out strolling on the Porth Hellick beach on St Mary's on 22 October 1707, the surprise was Sir Cloudesley Shovel, Admiral of the Fleet, whose flagship, HMS *Association*, was wrecked on the Gilstone Rock along with three other ships, and two thousand men were lost. Sir Cloudesley was miraculously still just alive, so she promptly murdered him for his emerald rings.

Spotting the porpoise took me back into the world of the *News Chronicle I-SPY* books, especially No. 1 in the series, *I-SPY at the Seaside*. I still have my original collection of *I-SPY* books, carefully concealed in a secret dossier, improvised from a cigar box, labelled: 'Private and Confidential – *I-SPY* Tribe'. I became an active Redskin around the age of seven, and the details of my sightings are carefully filled in with pencil. 'Going to the sea', says the introduction, 'is always exciting. But it's simply wizard when you are an I-SPY. Such a lot of things to look for – such fun putting them in your record! It's thrilling to see your score mount up.'

Back at the *News Chronicle* Wigwam in London, Big Chief I-SPY awarded points for each entry in your record book. For the rarer things you scored more than for those which were easily spotted. It is interesting to compare how rare or common things were perceived to be in the 1950s, compared to our present-day perceptions. In my *I-SPY Birds*, I find that the linnet and the song thrush score a mere twenty points, level pegging with the starling and the house sparrow. Both birds have suffered big declines in population over the last twenty-five years, and would probably rate more points now. In *I-SPY in the Country*, a grass snake scored a surprisingly low twelve, not much more than a frog, toad or scarecrow at ten, and less than a cattle grid at fifteen. An otter scored a mere twenty, at the same level as a road sign saying, DANGER THIS ROAD IS SUBJECT TO FLOODING, and only marginally more than a thatched pigsty at fifteen. (I have searched high and low for a thatched pigsty and I still haven't seen one.) One of the highest-scoring sightings in *I-SPY at the Seaside* was, in fact, the porpoise or dolphin. Both scored a princely forty, and it was time to open the Tizer if you saw one. The dolphin, according to *I-SPY*, is 'a very fast swimmer, and can move through the water quicker than you can scoot along the road on your cycle'. According to the book, I saw my first porpoise swimming in a school off Portrush on 20/4/54. I spotted my lugworm on 17/9/53 at Eastbourne.

Big Chief I-SPY always ended his messages to us Redskins with the coded message 'Odhu/ntinggo'. If you're a Paleface, I'm afraid you'll have to work it out for yourself. I wish I could help, with my copy of *I-SPY Secret Codes*, but it is Private and Confidential and 'Redskins are enjoined to keep this book in a safe and secret place.'

Masses of wild flowers grew everywhere in this Bronze Age landscape of ancient tracks, hedges, stone walls and tiny bulb fields, nearly all of which were now abandoned, grazed or cut for hay. None of them was more than a half or quarter of an acre and they were full of celandines, bluebells, wild garlic, violets and daisies, as well as leftover daffodils. The islands' traditional flower-growing economy was killed off mainly by the Dutch, who now cultivate everything under glass all the year round. Instead, there is tourism, and the wild flowers abound. Sea cabbage and rock campions line the shore, and pennywort grows from the stone walls. A pair of cows in a paddock munched at their plastic bucket beside five hundred lobster pots and an old Rayburn cooker. The blackbirds were trusting and unafraid.

Down at the southern end of the island I swam in Rushy Bay, a delightful sheltered sandy cove which looks across to Samson. It was completely deserted and I crossed from one side of the bay to the other. The intensity of the sky, the white sand, and the rocks that stood up everywhere out of the sea, had a dream-like quality reminiscent of Salvador Dali. Further out, puffs of light breeze squiffed the sea into little Tintin wavelets with kiss-curl tops. Someone had been here earlier; I found a number of elaborate sand and pebble mazes, one with the caption written with a stick: 'A Scilly Maze'. They too had a distinctly Bronze Age look to them. As I swam out, I pondered the mazes, and a theory John Fowles proposes in the book *Islands* that a pebble maze across the water on St Agnes was originally constructed by Viking visitors, or even a Phoenician sailor two and a half thousand years ago. Such ancient mazes are quite common in Scandinavia, but their ritual significance is a mystery. Fowles thinks it may have been connected with the grave, and escape into reincarnation. He also thinks Shakespeare imagined the maze-like *Tempest* in the Scillies. Drifting ashore again over the seaweed and sand, I wondered how many shipwrecked sailors had landed here, alive or drowned. If there were mermaids anywhere in the world, they must be here.

I walked back past another maze – of tall hedges of escallonia, senecio and pittosporum, a New Zealand immigrant that does well here in the frost-free conditions and provides belts of shelter from the Atlantic storms for the flower crops. Back in the Fraggle Rock Café for dinner, Les, the proprietor, said she and a gang of her friends originally came to Bryher to live twenty years ago as hippies. They weren't the first. In AD 387, a couple of early Christian bishops called Instantius and Tibericus came to the Scillies and founded a cult of free love well away from the hurly burly of the Dark Ages.

Bryher has a wonderfully relaxed approach to tourism, with little children's stalls outside some of the low garden walls offering painted stones or big pink and purple sea urchin shells for sale for pence left in a Tupperware box. There is an all-pervading sense of a Whole Earth Catalogue culture of improvisation and mixed economics. I recognised it straight away and warmed to it. It reminded me of a time, not long ago, when money was not the main topic of conversation. The Bryher lobster pots, I noticed, are built on a foundation of a steel boot-scraper doormat, with a tented framework of half-inch blue alkathene water-pipe covered in netting, and a funnel entrance improvised from a plastic flowerpot.

The looting of wrecks continues to be an important component of the island economy. There are people who can get you almost anything, depending on the nature of the latest cargo to be washed ashore or upended on the rocks. The current treasure trove was a container ship called *Cita*, wrecked off St Mary's and something of a floating department store for the jubilant islanders. Suddenly every household had a brand-new car battery, plastic toothbrush-holder (a choice of yellow, pink or blue), new stainless-steel sink, several bottles of Jack Daniel's, and a mahogany front door. This information suddenly made sense of the abundance of mahogany front doors lying about in front gardens, slightly frayed at the corners from their adventures at sea, some already installed incongruously in cottage doorways, garden sheds and extension conservatories. All of this, of course, was in strict contravention of the Merchant Shipping Act 1995, Part ix, Section 236, which obliges you to report any cargo you find from a wrecked vessel to the Receiver of Wreck. Forms for the purpose are available from Falmouth, just a two-day journey away on the ferry.

The delight of Bryher is that nowhere on an island a mile and a half long is more than half an hour's walk away. I went over Shipman Head Down to the cliffs above Hell Bay to watch the Atlantic sunset. There were convenient plump cushions of sea pinks on every ledge, and I watched the rocks gradually surfacing like bared teeth as the tide fell. I find sunset more dramatic than dawn because you know the spectacle is going to improve as it reaches a climax. The sun dropped like a billiard ball over the rim of the known world in due splendour, and I was watching from the front row.

I was piped awake early by the oystercatchers next morning, and set off along one of the sandy island paths to Green Bay, facing east towards the island of Tresco. It is more sheltered here, and there were boats pulled up on chocks for repair, and a boatbuilder's shed. Around it, near the shore, was a dazzling semi-natural colony of plants that must have originated in the tropical gardens at Tresco: dark blue aechium (which can grow nearly a foot a week), bright yellow aeolium, banks of blue agapanthus, and creeping masses of the colourful succulent osteospermum.

I went down to the beach for a swim in the Bronze Age fields. The Scilly Isles are the last outcrop of a ridge of volcanic granite that forms the backbone of Cornwall and they were, until about 4,000 years ago, the high points of one big island called Ennor. But the melting of the polar ice caps that began after the last Ice Age meant that Ennor's lowland valleys and fields were gradually submerged by the rising sea.

I donned the wetsuit, mask and snorkel, and swam out into the shallow sandy bay. It was high tide and about thirty yards off the shore I looked down at a pair of stone walls meeting at a right angle, and a circle of stones that must once have been a sheep pen. With seaweed hedges growing from the stones, these are the patterns and remains of the patchwork of old fields that once stretched all the way across the valley to Tresco. They are really just a continuation of the remaining field boundaries on shore. This may be why some stretches of water around the Scillies still have names from Before the Flood that are literally outlandish, like Garden of the Maiden Bower, or Appletree Bay.

As I swam back and forth across the bay, face-down in the clear salt water, searching out the diagonals of more old field walls, lulled by the rhythm of my own breathing amplified in the snorkel, I felt myself sinking deeper into the unconscious world of the sea, deeper into history. I was going back 4,000 years, soaring above the ancient landscape like some slow bird, and it reminded me how like the sea a field can be; how, on a windy day, silver waves run through young corn, and how a combine harvester can move through barley like an ungainly sailing vessel. I imagined ploughmen with seagulls in their wake tilling these fields, and their first flooding by a spring-tide storm, the crops ruined and the earth poisoned by the salt. The relation between the remaining fields and these that were submerged is an intimate one. Much of the island topsoil is composed of centuries of seaweed, forked into carts at low tide and flung about as a mulch. The molluscs, of course, were all quite at home on the stones of the sunken walls, and the winkles could have been so many land snails.

I was struggling out of the wetsuit on the beach when I noticed a bumblebee fly straight out over the sea towards Tresco. Three more took the same line of flight and I tracked them well out along the three-quarter-mile journey to the next island. Tresco has some famous gardens which would be highly attractive to bees, but Bryher was hardly short of flowers. Was this, I wondered, some ancient flight path used by bees 4,000 years ago and somehow imprinted in the collective bee memory? Or had some ambitious forager scented flowers on Tresco and blazed the trail? Along the tidemark were thousands of the most beautiful miniature shells, all much the same snail design but coloured russet, orange, peach, white, speckled, grey and silver. Each of them might have represented one of the drowned sailors whose spirits crowd the seabed of the Scillies.

Next afternoon I boarded the *Scillonian* and rode the Atlantic swell back to Penzance. A party of men with deep tans, pony-tails and expensive manly footwear with miles of bootlace, dotted themselves about the deck, bagging all the suntraps, and sat with their backs to the funnel or a life-raft, eyes shut, heads back, wearing beatific expressions. (They were met later at Penzance by waving women in jodhpurs and Range Rovers.) I sat against my rucksack, gazed down the snowy wake, and entered my own reverie.

3

Lords of the Fly

THE MOMENT I arrived in Stockbridge I scented water. And when I switched off the engine, I heard it. Arriving by car seemed all wrong. I should have been tethering a horse, or handing him over to an ostler. The place has an air of faded gentility, dominated by the rambling Grosvenor Hotel halfway along a main street that must be at least thirty yards wide, like a scene out of the Wild West. Before the 1832 Reform Act, this modest village returned two members of parliament, who had of course paid for the privilege. It was a classic rotten borough. There's an old Georgian rectory with two enormous magnolias either side of the front door, and the most beautiful country garage in all England. It still sells petrol from the original pumps. With perfect timing, a Morris Minor pulled up just as I was admiring the festive red-white-and-blue painted doors and a balcony festooned with geraniums to match, growing in suspended tyres.

The village is a riot of small rivers, a rural Venice. Half a dozen different streams, all purporting to be the authentic Test, flow under the wide main street and emerge to gossip through the hinterland of gardens, paddocks, smallholdings, toolsheds, old stables and outhouses behind the facade of shops and cottages. The gurgling of fast-flowing water is everywhere, and mallards wander the streets at will, like sacred cattle in India. Their ducklings are regularly swept away on the rapids, so there is always the poignant dialogue of orphans and bereaved mothers to strike anguish into the heart of the passing traveller.

How marvellous to find a place that values, uses and enjoys its river like this, instead of tucking it away out of sight, corseted in a concrete pipe. Stockbridge has made the most of the Test in a hundred different ways. And everywhere there are trout, as there are cats in the night streets of Istanbul. Renowned as the finest chalk stream in the world, the Test is a fly-fishing Mecca, home of the august Houghton Fishing Club. The fishing rights along these hallowed banks quietly change hands at over £1 million a mile and a day's sport on the Test can cost as much as £800. If they caught me swimming in their river, these people might cheerfully have me for breakfast, poached, with a little tartar sauce. But there are no greater connoisseurs of fine fresh water than our native brown trout, and I was determined to share with them the delights of the Houghton Club waters.

Five minutes out of the village down a waterside path, I was alone in the meadows on the brink of a wide, cold-water swimming hole, scene of the noisy reunion of the wandering offspring of Mother Test. Slightly to my surprise, there were no fishermen about, so I hurled myself straight in. The water made me gasp. The colder it is the better trout like it, because water's oxygen content rises as the temperature drops. (This is why there is such a super-abundance of marine life in the oceans nearest the poles.) I crossed a gravelly bend, swimming across the current into the confluence, a pool screened with bullrushes along the far bank. Some early swallows swooped low over the water. Squadrons of shadowy trout darted against the pale, stony bed creating bow-waves as they sped away. I turned and glided downstream, brushed by fronds of water crow-foot that gave cover to the trout as well as to the nymphs of the mayflies that would soon emerge to seduce them. No wonder trout love the Test. It is fast, startlingly clear, and alternates between riffling shallows and deeper pools. The bottom is chalky gravel with the odd worn brick. And there's plenty of cover.

Long Pre-Raphaelite tresses of water buttercup belly-danced in the current. I anchored myself on the weed, buoyed by the racing stream, then swam two hundred yards downstream to a peaty bay where the cattle come to drink. One side was kept clear of trees and vegetation to give a clear run to the rods, with all the cover on the opposite bank. A romantic-looking couple in their sixties passed by through the meadow and we exchanged a polite 'good afternoon'. They did their best to look unsurprised. Growing acclimatised, or numbed, I swam on, expecting at any moment to encounter a fly-fisherman knee-deep in waders, wondering what on earth I would say if I did.

THE FOLLOWING MORNING, ten miles to the east in Winchester, I ran into a swarm of reporters outside the Crown Court for the opening of the re-trial of Bruce Grobbelaar, Hans Segers and John Fashanu on charges of fixing the results of football matches for the benefit of some Far-Eastern betting syndicates. Photographers milled about, waiting for Grobbelaar and Co. to arrive. There was excitement in the air, and I couldn't resist slipping into the gallery of Court 3 with the assorted hacks covering the story. At least twelve wigs busied themselves around the court, as well as numbers of clerks, and I mused on the cost of it all. The first trial had collapsed because the jury couldn't reach a verdict. They had found the evidence incomprehensible. Addressing the jury, the judge referred with relish to 'the vast files of papers which are available to us all'. Counsel for the prosecution told them: 'Parts of the story are, dare I say it, quite exciting. Others are extremely turgid.' You could say that again. The interesting bits were the bizarre details about the business lives of these footballers. Fashanu's company, Fash Enterprises, had its offices at Warm Seas House, St John's Wood. Grobbelaar's company was the Mondoro Wildlife Corporation Ltd.,

Mondoro being, the court was helpfully informed, the Shona word meaning 'Lion God'. Nothing like this ever happened in swimming, I naively thought at the time. The furore over the allegedly doped-to-the-gills Chinese team at the Australian games was yet to come. So were similar accusations against the Irish Olympic champion swimmer Michelle Smith and her trainer-husband Erik de Bruin.

I soon adjourned to René's Patisserie for breakfast, and followed that with a reconnaissance of the main object of my visit, the Itchen, one of William Cobbett's favourite rivers. Cobbett loved every inch of the Itchen Valley, from the source at Ropley Dean near Alresford all the way to the sea at Southampton. 'This Vale of Itchen', he writes in *Rural Rides*, 'is worthy of particular attention. There are few spots in England more fertile or more pleasant; and none, I believe, more healthy.' Even by Cobbett's time, Winchester was 'a mere nothing to what it once was' – a place of residence for the Kings of England. But it still has King Arthur's round table in the Guildhall next door to the court where the three errant footballers stood trial. And it still has the Winchester College water meadows, where Izaak Walton must have fished in his later years while stay-ing with his daughter Anne. He died in Winchester in 1683. When I asked my way to the meadows in a bookshop, the proprietor said: 'Let's step outside and I can direct you with more gusto.'

I approached the river through narrow streets lined with college houses and SILENCE – EXAMS notices. The teachers all seemed to live in some splendour, in period town houses like Mill Cottage, approached through a small latched gate and a white wrought-iron footbridge across a mill-race. Roses over the door, a tortoiseshell cat curled by the milk-bottles, and the morning paper half in the letterbox completed the picture. The banks of the little stream, a branch of the Itchen, were decorated at intervals with PRIVATE – NO ACCESS notices. In another of these houses, almost next door to the college porters' lodge, an advertisement on a postcard in the window caught my eye: STONE HOUSE DATING FROM 11TH C. IN CRESPIANO NEAR FIVIZZANO, LA LUNIGIANA, MASSA CARRARA, ITALY. 9–12 ROOMS, 3 FLOORS. 100,000,000 LIRE = £36,000 ETC. This contrasted with another window card I had noticed earlier up in the town: A WHITE HOM MADE TEDDY BEAR WITH WHITE TROUSERS £6.50.

The pathos of this affected me all day. This was a city of such contrasts; the bishop in his palace, the footballers investing huge sums in their offshore enterprises, a gardener in a 'Madness' T-shirt circling on an Atco mower round a mulberry in the college grounds, the invisible students at their exams, the teddy-bear maker coaxing the tailored white trousers over the chubby legs.

Approaching the Itchen along College Walk, I came eventually to the water meadows and two or three piebald horses grazing by the river. I vaulted a low fence, steadying myself on a PRIVATE FISHING notice, and crossed the meadow to a convenient willow, where I changed into bathing trunks and a pair of wetsuit boots for the return journey from my swim, and sank my rucksack and clothes into a patch of nettles. At the chalky, gravel bank I confirmed Cobbett's observation, made on 9 November 1822, that: 'The water in the Itchen is, they say, *famed* for its *clearness*.' I plunged into the river, which was three to four feet deep, with here and there a shallow, sandy bank cushioned by water crowfoot. The current was fast enough to make it slow going if I turned and struck out upstream. But I rode downstream with the river in a leisurely breaststroke, keeping my eyes open for whatever might be round the next bend. I was rewarded with the sight of a water vole crossing over and disappearing into the reed-bed on the far bank. The river swung round in a long arc through the water meadows, and very sweet it was too. Here and there I saw the dark forms of trout, and minnows hung in the sandy riffles. This was very fine swimming, and I continued downstream towards the places once known as Milkhole and Dalmatia, where the Winchester College boys used to swim. The Itchen is fed at intervals by natural springs, which is why there are watercress beds along the valley. At Gunner's Hole, a fabled bathing pool further upstream which I intended to explore in due course, the springs are said to create dangerous undercurrents from time to time, and in the early part of this century a boy was drowned there. What the college now calls 'proper swimming' only began in 1969 when an indoor pool was built.

Breaststroking softly through this famously clear water I was soon dreaming of the strawberry garden at the family seat of the Ogles at Martyr Worthy upstream, thus described by Cobbett:

> A beautiful *strawberry garden*, capable of being *watered*
> by a branch of the Itchen which comes close by it, and
> which is, I suppose, brought there on purpose. *Just by*,
> on the greensward, under the shade of very fine
> trees, is an *alcove*, wherein to sit to eat the strawber-
> ries, coming from the little garden just mentioned,
> and met by bowls of cream coming from a little
> *milk-house*, shaded by another clump a little lower
> down the stream. What delight! What a terrestrial
> paradise!

I had climbed out of the river and was strolling back through the lovely water meadows still far away in my day-dream, milkmaids plying me with laden bowls of fresh strawberries and cream, when a *shout* rudely intruded on my pink and brown study: 'Do you realise this is private property?' The horses looked up for a moment and resumed their grazing. I decided to ignore the two irate figures on the fenced footpath and pressed on with all dig-nity in my bathing trunks towards the hidden clothes in the nettle patch. It crossed my mind to make my escape across the water, but then I thought of Cobbett and what he would have done, and that settled it. I was going to stand up for my rights as a free swimmer.

I got changed as languidly as possible, then casually

leapfrogged the fence and sauntered off along the path, whistling softly to myself, as an Englishman is entitled to do. 'Excuse me,' came a voice, 'does that fence mean anything to you?' This was unmistakable school talk, and I turned round to confront two figures straight out of Dickens; a short and portly porter with a beard and Alsatian, and a gangling figure on a bike with binoculars, strawberry-pink with ire, the College River Keeper. I introduced myself and enquired the cause of their disquiet. They said the river was the property of the college, and full of trout for the pleasure of the Old Wykehamists who sometimes fish there. It was definitely not for swimming in by *hoi polloi*.

'But the ladies in the public library told me the whole of Winchester used to swim in the river here right up to the 1970s,' I said.

'That's just the problem,' they replied. 'A few years ago we had six hundred people coming from the town, swimming in the river, eroding the banks and leaving litter behind.'

It sounded like paradise to me.

'But surely,' I said sweetly, 'we should all have access to swim in our rivers just as we should be free to walk in our own countryside. Don't they belong to all of us?'

The River Keeper practically fell off his bike. The porter flushed a deeper strawberry and allowed the Alsatian a little closer to my person. They both looked pityingly at me.

'There's plenty of coast and sea not far away if you want to swim,' ventured the porter.

At this point things suddenly turned nasty. They accused me of scaring away the trout and the porter muttered about calling the police. I said stoutly, and perhaps unwisely, that if I frightened away the fish, which I doubted, perhaps I was doing them a good turn, since if they stayed they would only be murdered by the Old Wykehamists. I told them I swim in the Waveney all the time in Suffolk in a place where bathers and anglers have co-existed happily for at least a century. And anyway, I said, why not designate one stretch of river for bathing and another for the Old Wykehamist fly-fishermen?

'We couldn't possibly do that because the water quality is too dodgy,' said the porter. 'Upstream of here they spray pesticides on the watercress beds and there's a sewage works discharging what should be clean water, but isn't always, into the river.'

I quoted Cobbett to them on the famously clear water. They laughed. There was no sign of the police, but the porter urged me to go away immediately and have a shower with plenty of hot water and soap to wash off all the pollutants in the river. People had been getting skin rashes, he said. Wishful thinking on his part, I fancied.

'But if the water is so evil and polluted, why aren't the trout all dead?' I asked. 'And why have you fenced in this footpath in a straight line miles away from the river instead of letting people enjoy winding along the lovely banks? Isn't that a bit mean?'

'I'm not wasting any more time with this,' he said, and

flounced off, the Alsatian casting hungry looks over its shoulder.

The episode raised some serious issues about swimming in the wild, if you can call Winchester wild. I reflected again on Cobbett, and how upset he was at the hanging of two men in Winchester in the spring of 1822 for resisting the game-keepers of Mr Assheton-Smith at nearby Tidworth. What they did amounted to little more than I had just done, yet I had not, in the end, been marched, dripping, up the hill to join Grobbelaar and Co. in the dock. Things were changing in Winchester, but only slowly. The truth was, I had enjoyed my row with the water bailiffs very much. I already felt invig-orated after a really first-class swim, and now I felt even better after a terrific set-to. But it seemed sad, and a real loss to the city, that the college no longer allowed swimmers in the river, or picnickers on the water meadows. I was left feel-ing very much like the otter, 'trapped but not detained', by one of the Houghton Club keepers in December 1853.

THE MATTER OF ownership of a river is fairly simple. Where a river runs through private land, the riparian owner also owns the river itself. On the question of access, the key legislation is the 1968 Countryside Act, which deliberately defined riverside and woodland as 'open country' in addition to the 'mountain, moor, heathland, cliff, downland and foreshore' originally listed in the 1949 National Parks and Access to the Countryside Act. 'River-side' includes the river as well as the banks in the definition of the Act. So whenever politicians mention 'open country' they are talking about rivers and their banks, as well as all those other kinds of countryside such as mountains and moorland. And when the Labour Party Policy Commission on the Environment promised, in July 1994, 'Labour's commitment to the environment will be backed up with legally enforceable environmental rights: a right of access to common land, open country, mountain and moorland,' they meant rivers and river banks too.

On the very same day as my Winchester fracas, Chris Smith, the Secretary of State for National Heritage, had been saying: 'I look forward, as Heritage Secretary, to working in partnership with the Ramblers' Association to secure access to open country, mountain and moorland for the ordinary people of Britain. Let's make a "right to roam" a reality!' So how about the right to swim? That so many of our rivers should be inaccessible to all but a tiny minority who can afford to pay for fishing 'rights' is surely unjust? I say 'rights' to point up the paradox, that something that *was* once a natural right has been expropriated and turned into a commodity. Fishing rights are only valuable because individuals have eliminated a public benefit – access to their rivers – to create an artificial private gain. The right to walk freely along river banks or to bathe in rivers, should no more be bought and sold than the right to walk up mountains or to swim in the sea from our beaches. At the moment, only where a river is navigable do you have rights of access along its banks.

That so many of our rivers should be inaccessible to all but a tiny minority who can afford to pay for fishing 'rights' is surely unjust?

In a recent survey of public opinion, the Countryside Commission discovered that one in three of all the walks people take in Britain involves water, or waterside, as a valued feature. In April 1967, a government official drawing up the 1968 Countryside Act observed:

> We have received a considerable volume of representations that the present arrangements for securing public access and providing a right of public passage on waterways is inadequate. In our opinion the solution lies in extending the powers to make access agreements or orders to rivers and canals and their banks . . . and we would propose therefore to extend the definition of open country to include these categories.

The flaw in the 1968 Countryside Act turned out to be that it relied on giving local authorities powers, but not *duties*, to create more access to rivers and their banks. Making voluntary agreements with private landowners could still work, if only the local authorities put more energy into it, and if only the landowners didn't have such enormous vested interest in the lucrative fishery. The government now says it will 'seek more access by voluntary means to riverside, woodland and other countryside as appropriate'. There is plenty of scope for such schemes: if all the river banks in Buckinghamshire were opened for public access, it would double the total length of footpaths

in that county. Riverside access is extremely popular. Perhaps we should learn from New Zealand, where they have
renewed a law originally enacted by a colonial governor at
the request of Queen Victoria. 'The Queen's Chain' gives a
twenty-two-yard strip of public access along the bank of
every river in the land. Across the Channel in Normandy
and Brittany, too, people have unlimited access to the
rivers.

The Environment Agency, meanwhile, is being influ-
enced by the powerful vested interests of the riparian
owners into confusing the natural value of chalk rivers like
the Itchen and the Test with their commercial value. It is
allowing them to be managed exclusively for the benefit of
trout fishery along much of their length. What were once
richly varied wild trout rivers have been allowed to become
highly manipulated leisure enterprises capable of deliver-
ing a more or less guaranteed catch of four or five fish to
the people, often tourists, who can pay to fish there. Trout
fisheries also persecute the pike, culling coarse fish by
electro-fishing, even removing such essentials to the ecol-
ogy of natural chalk streams as brook lampreys and
bullheads. Besides all this, they cut and remove the weed
that would otherwise naturally hold up the flow and
maintain the depth of water, as well as harbouring the
invertebrates that provide vital food in the rivers' ecosys-
tems. On one short stretch of the Test above Whitchurch,
the owner deploys over sixty different traps for stoats and
weasels along the banks, which tend to be manicured of

their natural cover with strimmers to accommodate the fastidious new breed of angler. What is at stake is the very resource that, left alone, would create and sustain the wild trout: the natural chalk stream.

Crayfish were once so abundant in the Itchen that when the river keepers cleared gratings and sluices along Winchester College water meadows, there would be dozens of them amongst the weed. But a few years ago the fish farms upstream introduced the American crayfish. The new arrivals carried a fatal disease, the crayfish plague, to which they, but not our native species, had developed immunity. The result has been the near-extinction of the wild crayfish from the Itchen. They are now reduced to a few isolated populations in side-streams or backwaters, having been replaced by their American cousins.

Now that the coast was clear again, I sauntered along the footpath across St Stephen's Mead, in search of the once-popular college bathing hole, Gunner's Hole. It was called after the Rev. H. Gunner, one of the college chaplains. There used to be a wide arc of changing sheds following the curve of the river bank, thatched huts on an island, and a system of sluices to regulate the natural flow of the water. Gunner's Hole was about a hundred yards long and twelve yards wide, and the stretch of river was dredged of mud and concreted along its banks towards the end of the nineteenth century. It even had a handrail around the area of 'a high diving erection with four stages and two springboards', as the *Public Schools' Handbook* called it in 1900, continuing enthusiastically: 'Gunner's Hole is now second to none as a bathing place in England. Here, under the shade of the limes, are the best features of a swimming bath and a river rolled into one.'

Sure enough, Gunner's Hole was still there, secluded under the shade of enormous plane trees and poplars, one or two now tumbled over the water. Its motionless surface was entirely covered by a classic duckweed lawn, the fabled disguise of Creeping Jenny, a monster of nursery folklore who would suck children under if they went too close, closing innocently over them to hide all trace of their fate. The massive concrete walls of the pool were in surprisingly good condition, and, on the basis that stolen fruit always tastes sweetest, I climbed through the concrete river inlet sluice to drop in silently at the deep end. Sinking through the opaque green cloak was like breaking the ice. I laboured down the hundred yards of the pool, mowing a path in the lawn which closed behind me as I went. Moorhens scampered off, half-flying over the billiard-baize green. The water beneath was still deep, but no longer the ten feet it used to be below the diving boards. It had silted up to between five and seven feet. Reaching down, I felt soft mud and ancient fallen branches, and sensed giant pike and eels.

Breaststroking back like a fly in soup, I reflected that Gunner's Hole must have been where one of the legendary sea-swimmers of our times evolved his style. Sir James

Lighthill was amongst the great mathematical scientists of the century. He became Lucasian Professor of Mathematics at Cambridge, and later Provost of University College, London. From Winchester he won a scholarship to Trinity College, Cambridge at the age of fifteen, and became a fellow at twenty-one. Lighthill was pre-eminent in the field of wave theory and fluid dynamics, and studied and analysed the pattern of the fierce currents that run round the Channel Islands. He was a strong swimmer, and put his knowledge to the test by becoming one of the first to swim the eighteen miles round Sark in 1973. By careful homework, Lighthill calculated the best course and timing to take advantage of the swirling, ferocious tides and currents. In ensuing years he returned and swam round the island five times. On his sixth island tour, in July 1998, aged seventy-four, he swam all day and was close to completing his nine-hour voyage when he ran into some rough seas. He was seen to stop swimming and died close to the shore. As was his custom, he was alone and had no boat with him. He regarded swimming as 'a most pleasant way to see the scenery', and swam on his back to conserve energy, describing his style as 'a two-arm, two-leg backstroke, thrusting with the arms and legs alternately'. I imagined the young Lighthill swimming up and down Gunner's Hole on summer evenings, perfecting his stroke, observing the complexities of the swimming style of the stickleback, and calculating distances.

There was no longer any sign of the diving boards or the

changing sheds, still marked on the 1953 Ordnance Survey map, but when I swam back to the concrete inlet I caught hold of a bit of the original handrail and climbed over into the fresh, fast water of the main river. In a metaphor for its history, Gunner's Hole used to carry the main stream, and is now a backwater. Dropping into a pool above the main sluice that controls the river level, I shed duckweed in a green confetti ribbon that went licking away on the stream. Standing chest deep, pinioned to the slippery wooden sluice gates whose grain stood out like corduroy, I imagined a future without fish farms or watercress beds, when the river could flow as sweetly as ever it did in Cobbett's day, and there could be bathing again in Gunner's Hole.

4

Tiderips and Moonbeams

Norfolk, 12 June

I SET OFF EARLY in a glowing dawn and drove on empty roads to the Norfolk coast, where I had arranged to meet Dudley, an old swimming and sailing companion. I could think of no better prospect than to enhance the day with bathing, walking and conversation on one of the best beaches I know. The journey through the rolling country-side of north Norfolk always feels to me like crossing over into another land, another state of mind. It is close to home, yet remote. The sudden lightness of being there, with such endless miles of level space, feels like a holiday, even for a few hours. Time passes slowly when you are a dot on the horizon. There is no anti-depressant quite like sea-swimming, and Holkham is where I usually go when I'm feeling sad. Striking out into the enormous expanse of cold sea, over the vast sands, I immerse myself like the fox ridding himself of his fleas. I leave my devils on the waves. North Norfolk is one of those places where the weather never seems to bear any relation to the forecasts. The whole of Britain can be covered in cloud, yet as you approach the coast up here, it is braided with a magic band of blue. The Royal Family must have known a thing or two when they chose Sandringham as a country cottage.

You arrive at Holkham beach as you would at Glyndebourne, Epidaurus or Newmarket races; there is a sense of occasion, as befits a visit to one of our most impressive stretches of wild coastline. Opposite the entrance to the Holkham estate you turn into a dramatic wide boulevard of poplars called Lady Anne's Walk and pay the Viscount Coke's amiable gatekeepers a modest sum to park. We felt we should be showing our passports. Even at this hour there were a couple of parked horseboxes with the ramps down, and a few Volvos with 'A dog is for life not just for Christmas' stickers in the back. This elegant cul-de-sac leads half a mile across the grazing marshes to a narrow gap in the Holkham Meals, the strip of mixed pine and holm-oak wood that runs along the dunes west to Burnham Overy Staithe and east to Wells.

Dudley and I set off barefoot over the sandy boardwalk through the wooded dunes and emerged blinking from the shade into the great gleaming theatre of Holkham Bay. A majestic sweep of dunes delineates an endless beach where, at low tide, the sea is only a distant whispering line of white. In the middle of all this are a couple of piratical sand islands that get cut off by the tide and are popular with lovers and picnic parties. Further west towards Burnham the dunes rise into a whale-back ridge reminiscent of the Malverns. There used to be the rusty hulk of an early Austin almost completely buried in the sand, but now I suppose it has sunk for ever, or dissolved. Coming along below the dunes was a string of twenty racehorses and their lads, returning to the horseboxes. It is the sort of thing you expect to see in Ireland, but there are often hoof-prints in the Holkham sand, and you can gallop for miles beside the sea.

We made for the surf across the almost deserted beach and half-waded, half-walked into the sun towards Scolt Head and Burnham Overy Staithe. One of the great joys of Holkham beach is to swim in the lagoons that appear in the sands as the tide goes out. Most are only just deep enough for a wallow, but some are up to four feet deep in places. They can be very warm, and I once stepped on a Dover sole in one. Miles from anywhere, we came upon a waterhole that was especially long and deep, and splashed about in it like two desert travellers in an oasis. Watching the little waves criss-crossing and buffeting each other, Dudley remembered how, as a boy learning to sail in Canada, he would study why this or that current behaved the way it did, or why there was a deep channel in the sand here but not there. Standing knee-deep in the sea and feeling it tug this way and that before we plunged out into deeper water, we agreed that these are indeed serious questions. Swimming into the sun, we struck out against the current. Our coast is being altered by the sea at every tide, and every storm, and nowhere more than here on the east coast. Back there on the beach I had searched for a whale jaw the size of an armchair that was stuck fast in the sand last winter, but was buried now, or washed away. Holkham is compulsive beach-combing. Razor shells are strewn everywhere like bones in a Mad Max film, and the delicate, finely perforated shells of sea urchins are beached like tattooed bums or paper masks.

Three miles on, by the entrance to Burnham Harbour, opposite Scolt Head Island, the channel buzzed with dinghies going in and out. Boats were pulled up on the beaches, and families picnicked in the dunes. I swam alone across to the island and back, dodging the Lasers and Enterprises. I felt the vigorous tug of the tide, and crossed the channel diagonally. If Nelson ever bathed, this would surely have been one of his haunts, close to his native Burnham Thorpe. But it was the policy of the navy to discourage and even forbid sailors to swim. Traditionally, few fishermen were swimmers either, the idea being that if you are going to drown in a shipwreck it is better not to prolong the agony.

We followed the path through Overy Marsh towards Burnham, passing two houseboats moored under Gun Hill. One was based on Noah's original drawings for the ark, with a single window facing west across the marsh. It bore a notice: 'This ark is used by a local artist as a simple working space. You are welcome to see inside when he is here. The only item of value inside is the Vieuw.' From the spelling, we deduced that Noah was Dutch. I could think of worse places to be stranded in the Flood.

A butterfly went past over the sea lavender. I said it was a swallowtail. Dudley thought it was a cabbage white. 'That's the difference between us,' he said. I kept my eyes firmly on the sandy path ahead, hoping to find a lizard out sunbathing. Dudley would probably think it was a stick, but I would know it was a lizard. We were, after all, in one of English Nature's prime reserves. There have been attempts to reintroduce the sand lizard here, but they have an uncooperative way of eating their own young. These dunes are also home to the natterjack toad, who likes to dig himself as much as a foot into the sand in the daytime, emerging at night to roam the flotsam line of the beach, hungrily rummaging the dead seaweed for the *Assiette de Fruits de Mer* of small creatures it contains.

Swimming into Burnham Overy Staithe on the mud-warmed rising tide, we entered a time warp. Sailing people sat about amongst the dinghies with picnic baskets and those Acme Thermos flasks finished in pale green Hammerite that weigh about the same as a milk churn. A woman in rust canvas shorts and plimsolls, with masses of fair curls like Titty in *Swallows and Amazons*, was fishing lifejackets out of a Land Rover Discovery. She told us that the channel through which we had just swum was known affectionately to the locals as Dead Man's Pool. They have

a way with metaphor in Burnham, always seeing in the
New Year round a bonfire of old boats.

A friend who has spent her springs and summers in
Burnham Overy Staithe all her life, once told me, 'I can
trace the creeks in the lines of my own hand.' We walked
back towards Holkham, navigating through waves of sea
lavender on the saltmarsh mud, crazed and frosted with
salt, until we reached the dunes again and ascended Gun
Hill, where I spotted a common lizard sunbathing oblig-
ingly before a clump of marram grass. The view into the
hazy distance of this great sweep of utterly wild coast
silenced us both for some time. Three miles inland we
could make out the elegant wooded landscaping of
Holkham Park, with its landmark obelisk and the fine
house well sheltered from the sea, looking out instead over
a lake. Holm oaks are the distinctive local tree here,
planted all over the estate by the pioneering agriculturalist
Coke in the eighteenth century. According to one of the
Holkham Hall gardeners, the trees first arrived as acorns
in a consignment of china from Italy. They had been used
as a kind of eighteenth-century bubblewrap, and Coke told
his men to fill their pockets with acorns in the mornings
and plant them all round the estate. Until Thomas Coke
built Holkham Hall in the middle of the eighteenth century, there had been almost no trees here at all, but, as the
historian David Dymond discovered, no fewer than
2,123,090 trees were planted on about 720 acres of the
park in the twenty years from 1781. It is interesting that

although the holm oaks and Scots pines, all planted by Coke, form a useful evergreen screen against the cold winds blowing in across the North Sea straight from the Ural Mountains of Russia, they also hide it from view. It is only relatively recently that we have come to regard a view of the sea as a thing of beauty. For our ancestors, the sea was to be feared and shunned from sight. When Humphry Repton designed Sheringham Hall, or 'Bower', further along this coast, in 1812, he positioned it facing east of south, away from the sea, only three-quarters of a mile away. He thought that 'A view of the sea . . . ought not to be the first consideration.'

A little further on, we were greeted by a sign, courtesy of English Nature, informing us that 'Naturists are requested to keep to the beach. Naturism is not permitted in the woods, or outside designated areas within the dunes.' Curious about the 'designated areas', Dudley and I headed straight off in search of them.

There is nothing quite so good as the feeling of hot sand sifting between your toes as you walk along the tops of dunes. We followed an undulating ridge path through a deserted, silent dunescape. Surely there was nobody about? By and by we came to a little village of driftwood windbreaks built around the natural declivities in the dunes. Still no sign of life. There were stacked-up red, yellow and blue plastic fish trays signalling a desire for privacy and goodness knows what else. Then, one by one, heads began appearing over the parapets of what the poet Kit

Wright has described as 'lust bowls'. Just as suddenly, the heads bobbed out of sight again and the silence continued. It was like the Somme at midday. We were surrounded by dozens of humans in this superheated warren and they had all gone to ground. Nonetheless we felt observed. It was an odd feeling, which we readily exchanged for the freedom of the beach below. 'They're obviously much engrossed in their books,' observed my companion.

Hastening away in the general direction of the distant sea, we encountered another of English Nature's notices: MEMBERS OF THE PUBLIC ARE WARNED THAT THIS PART OF THE BEACH IS UNDER USE BY NATURISTS. The telling use of the words 'warned' and 'under use' made it quite clear that in the well-dressed offices of English Nature a naturist would be regarded with the same degree of alarm as an unexploded mine. Looking back from the beach towards the Somme as casually as we could, naked figures could be seen rising up from time to time out of the bunkers for surveillance purposes. It was like a scene from *Watership Down*. The Unclothed Ones were mostly male and very white, but a few varied in hue from underdone to deep Greek Island tan. Every now and again, in ones or twos, they would make the long trek across the beach to cool off in the sea. There was a distinctly erotic air to the place that some-how lent a restless, urban feeling to the wild and beautiful dunes, and put them out of bounds.

The noticeboards and the frisson of nudity about the dunes bespoke the continuing British confusion about bodies. Well into the nineteenth century, to go swimming was to go naked, especially in the wild. I have a print of a photograph, taken at the bathing-lake in Victoria Park, Hackney, in 1899, in which not a single one of literally hundreds of boys bathing is wearing a stitch, and there is not a girl in sight. Until halfway through the eighteenth century, people still swam in the sea principally for their health, but during the next fifty years they came to the beaches more and more for pleasure. The elaborate bathing machine was simply a recognition by the Victorians of the erotic potentialities underlying sea-bathing. Mention of the seaside was often the occasion for a nudge and a wink. The characteristically English obsession with swimming costumes and near-nudity was the *raison d'être* of McGill's seaside postcards. You find it in the heavy-handed humour of a letter, dated 1930, to the *Swimming Times*, on behalf of 'The Slow-butsure Breast Stroke Swimming Club of Wobbleham Village, Little Loweringham'. It is there, too, in the Amateur Swimming Association's edict, in the same year, that costumes 'must be non-transparent, shall be one piece, devoid of open-work, and reach within three-and-a-half inches from the base of the neck, back and front. In the leg portion, the costume shall be cut in a straight line round the circumference of each leg.' Even as recently as the 1997 World Championships in Australia, when Steve Zellen lost his trunks as he dived in at the start of a race and swam on, he was disqualified. (Arguing his case before the judges, he said he would have stopped had it been a backstroke event.)

English Nature's warnings alerting people to the possibility that a naturist might pass within their field of vision shared something of the comical quality, it seemed to me, of the Vatican's precautions, described in this cutting from the *Telegraph* I found recently on a friend's study wall:

VATICAN OBLIGES SHY SWAMI

Special arrangements of unusual rigour have had to be made at the Vatican over the weekend for the Papal audience of Pramukh Swami, an Indian spiritual leader, who has not seen a woman for 46 years. In order that he should not break this rule inadvertently in the Vatican of all places, women, including nuns, were kept away from the route as the 63-year-old Hindu monk was brought to the Papal palace and ushered into the Papal presence on Saturday. The sect's leader is accompanied by nine other monks and by a group of laymen whose special task it is to warn him in good time of the approach of a woman and then guide him with his eyes shut.

It was getting really warm, and, not to be outdone, we stripped off to wade and swim alternately in the general direction of Wells, accompanied by a posse of oystercatchers and several sandpipers, who scampered after invisible delicacies with desperate urgency as the tide went out, uttering little cries of discovery. We again felt the fierce undertow that runs along this coast, and the sea bottom was full of sudden dips and channels. Bathing off this beach, you feel the literal meaning behind Larkin's line about misery in 'This Be the Verse': 'It deepens like a coastal shelf.' I thought of the two children, brother and sister, who had drowned a few miles away, at Holme-next-the-Sea a year or so earlier. The family had been picnicking on the wide beach and the children had wandered off to play or paddle in the far-off sea. Their parents suddenly realised they had lost sight of them and began the increasingly desperate search. In line with contemporary fears about paedophiles, much of the anxiety and police attention focused on the possibility of abduction, at the expense of what some might consider the far more obvious danger: the sea. Nobody will ever know what actually happened that day, but it is likely that the children paddled innocently into the warm, inviting shallows, only to stumble into one of those sudden troughs in the sand and find themselves in deep water, clutched by the riptide. In the space of two weeks they were to be carried thirty-four miles round the coast to the beach at Sheringham by the same powerful sea current that sweeps south down the whole east coast of this island, bringing ever more pebbles to the great shingle bank at Blakeney Point.

There were places where the current tugging at our legs almost stopped us wading, and where swimming would not have been a good idea. Whenever we swam, we noticed how much we drifted. Like the currents, waves behave differently all along this beach, and we came to a place where people were vigorously body-surfing into the shallows. I thought of Byron, who 'wantoned' in the breakers in Italy at Lerici. We threw ourselves into the naked buoyant tumbling, and gloried in the abandonment in wave after wave, happy as the bathing pigs of Kythnos we had once discovered.

We had been sailing across the Aegean in a small wooden sloop, heading for the harbour at the northern end of Kythnos, but were blown so far off course by the Meltemi that we almost missed the island altogether. Having just managed to claw our way around its southern tip into the shelter of a providential cove, we rode out an anxious night and awoke to rosy-fingered dawn and a perfect sandy bay. There was not a soul in sight. But the beach was not empty. In the shade of a tin shelter on driftwood stilts, occasionally strolling into the sea for a dip and a roll in the shallows, lolled a dozen ample sows. I hope those pigs still have the beach to themselves.

Heading back for tea at Holkham Hall, we followed the tracks of a pram which had been wheeled a mile across the sands. Amongst the big limes and oaks in the park there were roe deer and sheep, and on the higher fields, an abundance of partridges and hares. The estate is not normally artificially stocked with partridges, so their success must be ascribed to the habitat. There has always been plenty of shooting on these Norfolk estates, but there are miles of good hedges too, the crucial factor for the breeding partridge. I had come across a copy of *The Shooting Man's Bedside Book* by 'BB' staying with some country friends. Holkham featured strongly in the chapter on record bags. It may not make ideal bedside reading for all of us, but on 19 December 1877 a shooting party of eleven killed 1,215 hares, and on 7 November 1905 a party of eight shot 1,671 partridge. It was a neighbouring estate, however, that took the prize for the Record Mixed Bag. At the end of a single day's shooting at Stanford on 31 January 1889, Lord Walsingham's party staggered in with an assortment of pheasants, partridges, red-legged partridges, mallard, gadwall, pochard, goldeneye, teal, swans, cygnet, woodcock, snipe, jack snipe, wood pigeon, herons, coots, moorhens, hares, rabbits, otter, pike and rat. A rare tribute to the biodiversity of north Norfolk.

Henry Williamson, the author of *Tarka the Otter*, loved the abundance and variety of living creatures in this countryside, and for seven years he lived and farmed five miles along the coast at Stiffkey. When Dudley returned home after tea, this is where I went, pitching my tent in a field that was once part of a wartime RAF camp, overlooking thousands of acres of wild saltmarsh, and Cabbage Creek. It is easy to get lost in this watery maze, and find yourself marooned on a rising tide.

From 1937, Williamson farmed 235 acres here, struggling to bring the derelict farmland back into good heart at Old Hall Farm. He recorded his day-to-day adventures in *The Story of a Norfolk Farm*, and in a regular column in the

Evening Standard which ran all through 1944 and '45, under
the title 'A Breath of Country Air'. He always left writing
the column until the last possible moment, and his two
little boys would be waiting in the kitchen, re-tying the
laces of their plimsolls ready for the sprint up Stiffkey
street to the post van at half past four. The poet of *Tarka*
bathed with his children in the warm water of the marsh
pools, often by moonlight, after as much as twelve hours'
prickly work in the harvest fields.

At dimmit-light, or dimsey, as they called twilight on
Tarka's River Taw in Devon (where Williamson lived before
and after Stiffkey), I went out over Stiffkey Marshes and
swam in the Stiffkey Freshes. A deep pink moon rose up
over Blakeney Point, whose bleached pebbles shone from
across the water. Although I couldn't see them, I knew there
were seals not far away on its outer beaches. A line of small
boats rode at their moorings out in Blakeney harbour.

I felt the tide running in as I entered the sea. It advanced
at astonishing speed, gaining three or four feet each minute, spilling over the almost level muddy sands in a rolling
three-mile meniscus that stretched unbroken all the way
west to Wells. The water was warming itself as it inched up
the wandering guts and channels where the sun had beaten
all day. It was calmed by the sheltering arm of the great
shingle bank opposite. I floated out into the freshes, the
water beyond the marsh, through bands of seaweed, letting myself drift with the tide along the strand towards the
mouth of the Stiffkey River, where there were houseboats,

half-hidden in the winding creeks, shuttered, silent and dark against the moon. I listened to the sea percolating into the marsh, sliding up every little meandering mud canyon, between the glidders and uvvers – the mud banks – trickling about the mycelium of creeks, gently rocking the glistening samphire. Even the tiniest channels in the mud or sand mimicked the patterns and movement of a great river.

As I bathed, I imagined Williamson, now an otter himself, swimming at dusk with nine children in one of the marsh pools, with the reflected wing-tip lights and the roar of the warplanes returning to the airfield behind Stiffkey. Then the air would be quiet again, as it was now, except for the cries and splashings of the children, and the marsh birds. The girls' clothes, draped over sea lavender, might well have included blouses or aprons of a fine red cotton, then the fashion in Stiffkey, because the 'mashes' were a popular children's hunting-ground for the much-prized scraps of the red drogue parachute targets, which were towed to and fro all day by aeroplanes, while gunners practised, filling the wide sky with black puffs of smoke.

When Williamson died, it was Ted Hughes who delivered the memorial address at the service of thanksgiving in St Martin-in-the-Fields. Hughes had found and read *Tarka* at the age of eleven and counted it one of the great pieces of good fortune in his life. For the next year he read little else. 'It entered into me,' he said, 'and gave shape and words to my world as no book ever has done since. I recognised even then, I suppose, that it is something of a holy book, a soul-book, written with the life-blood of an unusual poet.' Hughes regarded Williamson as 'one of the truest English poets of his generation', although he never published a word of verse. *Tarka* had taken four years to write, and went through seventeen drafts. Williamson rewrote Chapter Eleven, which begins at the source of five rivers up on Dartmoor, thirty-seven times. He described the writing of those paragraphs to Hughes as 'chipping every word off the breastbone'. The two men became friends when Hughes, not much over thirty, and still spell-bound by the magical book, found himself living in the middle of Devon on the Taw not far from where William-son, now in his sixties and also still under Tarka's spell, was working in a hut on a patch of land he had bought with the prize-money his book had won him long ago. (He had sold the Norfolk farm by the end of 1945, his dreams unrealised.)

I have always admired Williamson, not only for the beauty and ice-clear accuracy of his writing, but for the moral basis of his vision, which sprang from the natural world and his passionate concern to take care of it. In this, he was far ahead of most of his contemporaries. Hughes described Williamson at that service of mourning as 'a North American Indian dreamer among Englishmen'.

When I came out of the water, my shadow fell twenty feet along the shell-strewn shoreline. The moon was rising towards a thin band of mackerel cloud, and terns, duck and wading birds called to one another all over the marsh. Nothing much had changed since Williamson was here, driving his grey Ferguson tractor in a mackintosh tied up with baling twine, building his wooden tide-doors to keep the river from flooding his fields, and trapping eels in his ditches.

5

Borrow & Thoreau

North Wales, 14 June

I WENT TO WALES because the place is stiff with magic, because the Rhinog Mountains are something like a wilderness where I would be free to wander like pipesmoke in a billiard room, and with the kind of apparently random purpose with which the laughing water dashes through the heather, rocks and peat. I went there to be a long way from all the powerful stimuli Wordsworth said prevented us, these days, from doing any proper thinking. My only purpose was to get thoroughly lost; to disappear into the hills and tarns and miss my way home for as long as possible. If I could find a string of swims and dips, each one surpassing the last in aimlessness, so much the better. The great thing about an aimless swim is that everything about it is concentrated in the here and now; none of its essence or intensity can escape into the past or future. The swimmer is content to be borne on his way full of mysteries, doubts and uncertainties. He is a leaf on the stream, free at last from his petty little purposes in life.

I took my Great Uncle Joe's copy of George Borrow's *Wild Wales*, the account of a three-week walk across that country in the summer of 1854. Borrow, who was a great swimmer as well as walker, is in some ways insufferable. He never ceases to pose on the page as he posed in life, and his prose is generally heavier going than even the wildest of Wales. Nonetheless, in his grandiloquent fascination with history and language (he liked to call himself a 'word-master'), and in his genuine curiosity about the lives of country people and gypsies, he is hard to ignore, and wins you round in the end.

Borrow used to swim all over the Norfolk Broads, where he lived, all year round, and in the North Sea when he moved to Great Yarmouth. If he couldn't sleep, or was bored with the company at home, he would walk twenty-five miles to Norwich and, after a rest at his mother's house, tramp back. He was six foot three, with a mane of white hair and massive shoulders, and cut a striking figure in Great Yarmouth in his sombrero and long sheepskin coat, with his servant, Hayim Ben Attar, and his black Arab steed, Sidi Habismilk. In the summer of 1854, Borrow embarked on his Welsh walk carrying only a small leather satchel with 'a white linen shirt, a pair of worsted stockings, a razor and a prayer-book'. Great Uncle Joe had *Wild Wales* with him in Parkhurst prison on the Isle of Wight in 1892, where he was doing time at the age of twenty on the trumped-up charge that he was a dangerous anarchist. I have often imagined the young idealist reading the book in his prison cell, dreaming of the freedom of the open road and the hills.

The Rhinog Mountains stretch south along the coast for eighteen miles between Snowdonia and Barmouth Sands. It was to this trackless quarter that I drove from Stiffkey, arriving in the dark to camp by the sea on Shell Island, south of Harlech, where I had arranged to meet my cousin Adrian in the morning for the first day's walking and high altitude swimming.

We began by scrambling uphill from the Roman Steps, a haphazard stair of roughly flat stones that was once a trade route through the Rhinogs. We were aiming for the *llyns*, Welsh for tarns, higher up. Connoisseurs of these mountains like Adrian are used to the absence of paths, and after much toil we eventually hoisted ourselves level with the lofty Llyn Du. We looked across it to an almost sheer ascent of some 650 feet to the summit of Rhinog Fawr at 2,347 feet. A brisk wind coming up the mountainside off the sea ruffled the surface of the tarn, which must have been 350 yards long and half as wide. The immense shadow of the mountain rendered the water opaque and black. To judge by the almost vertical plunge of the mountain into the *llyn* on the far side, it must have been very deep. We were about 1,700 feet above the sea and feeling distinctly cool, even in our mountain gear. My companion began to shiver, and, lacking a wetsuit, decided to give this particular treat a miss.

This was a moment I had anticipated with relish. I slipped off a rock into the velvet deeps and swam suspended in what suddenly felt like giddy depth. It was icy. I swam straight out and across the middle of this chasm, gulping air and moving fast towards a sloping ramp of grey fissured rock at the far end of the ruffled tarn, entertaining the usual fantasies about what company I might have below. But it was still a beautiful swim, my feelings of awe intensified by the gothic mist. Adrian, who is Head of PE at a Gloucester comprehensive school, cut a reassuring figure across the water. The rock here is mostly Cambrian, a hundred million years old. The rock and the country are one and the same: Cambrian and Cambria. The two next oldest rocks, the Ordovician and the Silurian, are named after two tribes of ancient Britons who lived on the Welsh borderland.

Halfway across, I turned and swam on my back and confronted the dark presence of the mountain. I thought of the phrase 'deep as England' in Ted Hughes's poem 'Pike'. Wales may be yet deeper. I was a prehistoric creature in my glistening wetsuit, ready to be fossilised unless I kept moving. I scrambled on to the huge, grey, ramped rock at the far end, and slithered higher up it to enjoy the view for a few moments before the wind began to bite. I took a header back in off the rock, my highest dive yet. The imperative to keep moving kept my mind off the chilled water, and I soon acclimatised once I got into the rhythm of the breaststroke, urgent at first, until I began to relax. I doubt I would have had the nerve to attempt the swim had I been alone. It was far colder when I came out; this was no place to stand about with nothing on. Neither of us had any doubt that a warming assault on the summit of Rhinog Fawr should be our next move. The cloud had by now almost cleared, and views were opening up on all sides. Some chocolate, and we were off on a spiral route up the northern slopes of the mountain to reach the south-western ridge, and the summit. As we clambered up the last few feet of chaotic rock, the cloud was clearing, and there were views across the sea and up the coast to Anglesey, where the sun had come out, and along the other Rhinog mountains stretching south in line towards Barmouth Sands; Rhinog Fach, Y Llethr and Diffwys.

We now descended on a circular route to the next tarn, Gloyw Llyn, which winked at us from below. We followed a stream, at first a tentative rill amongst the rocks and tussocks, but soon growing into a fully-fledged torrent. Just as we were whingeing about the boggy going, and clambering round a series of minor waterfalls, we came upon a classic swimming hole. It was a verdant pear-shaped pool sheltered by a grassy bank to one side, with steep mossy rock rising out of it on the other, clothed in stunted gorse and tussocks. It felt warmer here, and we had both worked up a sweat. By now the sun was out, shining straight through the lens of water onto the golden peaty pebbles of the bottom. We stripped off and leapt in. It took our breath away. The pool was three or four feet deep with just enough room to swim, as in a treadmill, against the current. Every second was an eternity. Neither of us stayed in for longer than a minute but sprang out on the knife-edge between aching and glowing.

A buzzard circled overhead. It saw two figures bounding downhill over bog moss and cotton grass to the big tarn, Gloyw Llyn, now gilded by the sun. It watched them climb out on to an outcrop of rock, take off all the clothes they had only just put back on, and dive into the lake. As it soared higher into the sun, the bird observed the two pale, naked figures crossing and re-crossing the tarn, and diving far down off the rock several times into the deep, clear water. Then it drifted away across the mountain.

On the way down the mountainside we passed through an ancient grove of stunted oaks, the trees so encrusted with mosses and lichens they looked like old cheeses left in the fridge for too long. The second tarn had been more than twice the size of the first, and nearly as cold, and we still luxuriated in the after-effects of the soft, sweet-tasting water's rigour. It had provided the crowning swim of the day.

We returned to civilisation for dinner at the Victoria Inn at Llanbedr. It was the sort of place where Borrow might well have dined. To my sadness and his, Adrian had to return home that night. I was going to miss his wit as well as his pacemaking. 'Will there be anything else?' asked the waitress as she cleared our table. 'What would you suggest?' we enquired. 'Well, nothing really,' she said.

After supper I went back up the mountain and camped

at the top end of a lake, Llyn Cwm Bychan, on a little sheep-mown peninsula where the river enters it. It had been in such flood a couple of weeks earlier that it would have submerged my tent to a depth of three feet. When it rains hard here, the water simply cascades off the mountains. It would be a perfect spot for an early-morning swim. I lay for a long while by the moonlit lake, imagining Borrow here, reflecting on the convivial pleasures of the day.

I always dream a lot when I am camping, in the sweet repose that comes with exercise and physical fatigue. 'The dreams are getting obsessive and I don't even know if I should own up to them,' I put in my notebook. 'By now I am dreaming almost continuously of rivers, seas, tides and ponds.' Tucked up on my peninsula with the sound of the river vibrating through the turf, I dream I am swimming in a still, black canal overhung by a cobbled wharf with a high roof, like a pagoda. At one end of the wharf there are wooden lock gates in deep water, and beyond the gates is something, I don't know what, that needs retrieving. I am with my dream friend from childhood and the other members of my own version of the Famous Five. We are definitely trespassing. One of us is going to have to creep on to the wharf and plunge down under the lock gates to reach the other side. I am the one who dives and I swim down and down under the looming gates in the green water, but I never know what is on the other side because that is the moment I wake up.

I woke to the beginnings of a fine day and bathed in the

lake off my peninsula, swimming through lingering mias-mal mists rising off the surface. Thoreau describes Walden Pond at such a moment: 'As the sun arose, I saw it throw-ing off its nightly clothing of mist, and here and there, by degrees, its soft ripples or its smooth reflecting surface was revealed, while the mists, like ghosts, were stealthily withdrawing in every direction into the woods, as at the breaking up of some nocturnal conventicle.' It is a marvel-lously unconscious evocation of the kind of scene Courbet loved to paint, of women undressing to bathe.

Searching the map, I had seen some promising upland streams, a waterfall and a tarn, so I hiked off uphill through the bracken. There is so much of it in the Rhinogs that the sheep all carry it around on their coats like camouflaged soldiers. I watched a ewe standing between two big rocks the shape of goats' cheeses. They were just far enough apart to allow the animal in, and I began to understand the relationship Henry Moore perceived between sheep and stones. He saw sheep as animate stones, the makers of their own landscape. By grazing the moors and mountains they keep the contours – the light and shade – clear, sharp and well-defined, like balding picture-restorers constantly at work on every detail. The black oblongs of their pupils set deep in eyes the colour and texture of frog skin are like the enormous slate coffin-baths you see in the farmyards here; seven foot slabs of slate hollowed into baths. Quite why the farmers made such things is a puzzle, when there are natural baths and pools in every stream inviting you to 'wash away the night', William Morris's phrase for the morning ablutions of his questing knights in *The Water of the Wondrous Isles*.

I climbed up a *cribin*, or *moel*, a rounded rocky outcrop commanding a view of the valley, and settled down in a warm sheep hollow. Every tree up here has a hollow the size and shape of a sheep, the roots exposed and polished by generations of them hunkering down. I sat perched on the first of a series of tumps rising in succession up a ridge, their rocks rounded by cushions of turf. I was level with the tops of hawthorns, rowans and ashes that grew on the slopes and grassy hillocks. There was birdsong everywhere; the rising notes of pipits, like the turning of a rusty wheel, the mew of the buzzard as it spun into view. Redstarts flew from tree to tree, taking the line a slack rope would take slung between them. Economy in flight is what makes it graceful. Look at the swift, which hardly seems to move its wings at all, or the planing buzzard, ascending a thermal. The redstart flaps its wings just enough to get from A to B and always lands on the upward beat, under full control. Birds always land rising, coming up to a branch or ledge, never down.

I removed my boots and stretched out to enjoy the sun. The hollow-sounding ground was still damp and my glasses, left lying on it, soon steamed up. With my face close to the turf I observed a faint mist rising from clumps of tiny flowers peopled with tiny insects: yellow tormentil, stonecrop, sage, thyme, sorrel, bell heather, foxglove, innumerable grasses, mosses, twayblade and heath bed-straw (now rumpled bedstraw) where I had been lying.

Wandering further on amongst these tumuli, I came upon the entrance of a cave, with a dozen steam genies twisting out of it where hot sun played on its wet, peaty floor, well manured by the sheep that must squeeze in and shelter there. I got my head and shoulders in, and waited for my eyes to grow accustomed to the dark, then used the reflected sunshine in my watch, a tiny sun dancing about the walls, to see how far it stretched into the hill. The cave had filled up with centuries of sheep-shit and ran for at least fifteen or twenty feet in a perfect five-foot arch of slate, with the rotten remains of wood protruding from the walls. I could have entered on all fours, but there was something unappealing about the idea of crawling in wet sheep-shit. Was it a slate mine, a lead mine, or a tomb? There was a stone circle not half a mile away.

I found two more cave entrances close by, both nearly blocked with loose earth, guarded by brambles, thistles and foxgloves. This was *Rogue Male* country, practically unmapped, and unfrequented. I made a mental note that I could go to ground here, as the nameless protagonist of the thriller goes to ground in Dorset, in the event of some future political or personal crisis, living on berries and mutton, and communing with the weasels. Here, too, was a roofless, circular, stone-walled chamber and three more tunnels running into the hill from higher up. They were much easier of access, five feet wide and four feet high, well lined with slates which now dripped on me as I crept in and explored. Practically brushing my cheek, a wagtail flew off a nest of five pale speckled eggs hidden in a sage plant and a hart's-tongue fern near the entrance. I crept in some twenty feet until the shaft ran off to my right in utter darkness and I lost my nerve and retreated gingerly, suddenly fearful of the rock-fall that clearly hadn't ever happened in several hundred years.

There was no sign of these tunnels on the map, and I was content for them to remain a mystery. Indeed, it was infinitely preferable to me that they should not be on the map, and never should be. This was one of those magical places the people of northern Greece call *Agrafa*, 'the unwritten places'. They are the remote and secret places in the Pindos mountains, bordering Albania and Macedonia, that were deliberately left off the map by the inhabitants so as to avoid the imposition of taxes by the occupying Turks. Borrow would certainly have gone and knocked on the nearest farmer's door and demanded to know the full history of the earthworks. No doubt his curiosity was laudable, but it also often seems impertinent and condescending. He would ask total strangers what they thought of their landlord, whether their parents were still living, or about their religion. It says much for the civility of the Welsh country people that they always seemed to give him straight answers.

I had been following a tributary river of the lake uphill and now came to a meeting of the water. I took the left fork and followed a delightful little rushing brook about four feet wide that ran steeply over a series of waterfalls between two and ten feet high. It ran alongside a south-facing stone wall that acted as a sounding board for its song, a continuous chord composed of the deep notes made by the spouting of water into stone hollows and the descants of the shallower rapids. Thus serenaded, I cooled off in a pool below a waterfall, so shaped that I could lie facing the morning sun with the cascade on my shoulders. By angling myself further back, I could get the full, icy force of the water over the back of my head, a sensation more often associated with warm water and the hairdresser's chair, and utterly exhilarating. Behind the curtain of water I saw the secret green lushness of liverwort. The view over the whole bowl of mountains was magnificent, and I hadn't seen a soul all morning. Wedged in the rocks were some old split hazel fencing stakes or wattles, eroded almost to a wafer by the stream. Just the knots and sinews of the wood remained. I retrieved a half-melted chocolate bar I had left to solidify under the water and soon dried off in the warm sun.

My next swim was about a thousand feet up, below the mountain succinctly known as Clip, in the comparatively balmy waters of Llyn Eiddew-mawr overlooking the vast estuary sands of Porthmadog. The tarn must be half a mile long, and it was perfectly clear, with a brown peaty bottom shading into invisible depths. The sun had been shining on the water all day, and I swam across and back very comfortably, having warmed up on the ascent. By now it was tea-time, and I lay on the bank eating nuts, dates and biscuits, wondering if the tarn had ever contained the 'afanc'. This is a creature that reputedly once lived in the Welsh lakes. It was considered by Borrow to have been the crocodile, and by others to have been the beaver. Myth has it that Hu the Mighty, the inventor of husbandry and a leader of the ancient Cymru, drew out the afanc from the water with his team of four oxen and banished it. Certainly there would once have been beavers in Welsh lakes, and, at one time, crocodiles. Musing by just such a lake as this on his walk, Borrow felt sure that if its depths were searched, 'relics of the crocodile and the beaver might be found'. 'Happy were I,' he says, 'if for a brief space I could become a Cingalese, that I might swim out far into that pool, dive down into its deepest part and endeavour to discover any strange things which beneath its surface may lie.' I had swum out far, but I had not dived down. The afanc was possibly some kind of plesiosaur, a fifteen-foot creature resembling a crocodile, one of whose fossil skeletons was discovered in the summer of 1844 at Kettleness on the Yorkshire coast. It is now built into the wall of the Whitby Museum.

I hiked downhill along one of the enormous stone walls, some up to eight feet high, that thread across this rugged country. Their only logic seems to be aesthetic. Only the longer ones appear to do much, like mark a boundary, or keep sheep in or out. These walls are reputed to have been built by French prisoners of war from Waterloo, and enclose wide 'fields' on the hillsides and tops, perhaps sixty or a hundred acres at a time. The work must have been immense. Maintaining them is a life's work too. I couldn't help thinking of the hernia unit at the Harlech General Hospital. It must be a busy place on market day.

I could hear the sound of laughing water across nearly a mile of hillside, and could soon see it too, tumbling, white and sparkling, over a ramp of black rock thirty feet high, like a leaking castle. Feeling like a striptease artist by now, I hung my clothes over a bilberry and climbed up the falls to the top. Water was gushing and surging up through a moraine of massive boulders, then sliding down a forty-five degree slab of rock, black where it was wet, and purple where it was dry. Lying back against the sloping rock I let the water flood over me, then swam against the current in a substantial pool lower down. Water rushed about everywhere here, and amongst the remains of a settlement I found a spring inside a kind of stone temple covered in ferns. I went down to drink from it, and felt its atmosphere and power. The sense of a Delphic presence was so palpable, the Oracle might just have gone for lunch. The cottages had been tiny; no more than eight feet square. The walls of one were still standing, and its hearth, too. On the old track that led away downhill was the most luxuriant bed of wild thyme I have ever seen. None of the ruins were marked on the map at all, which only made discovering them the more thrilling.

I climbed into the river where it ran on through a miniature ravine full of the bright, rich pinks of heather, bracken, stonecrop, thyme, gorse and the little yellow tormentil. I followed it down through a ladder of waterfalls and pools, some of them deep enough to swim, interspersed with straight, high-speed runs between great slabs of rock. Here and there the stream would bend sharply to the left or right and the water would climb up the rock wall and spout into thin air like an eel standing on its tail. Then it merged with another stream, running down an almost parallel ravine, and I slid, scrambled, waded, swam, plunged and surfed through it all until I was delivered into a deep, circling pool. A little further on, a solitary sycamore stood sentinel over a sheep-nibbled lawn of buttercups and daisies by a waterfall and another pool, long and deep, between black slabs of rock, where I swam against the stream and hovered in the clear black water. Here I made my camp, hanging my towel to dry in the sycamore branches. I made delicious tea with the river water, devoured bread, goats' cheese and pennywort leaves, and fell into a deep sleep, lulled by the song of the waterfall, of Minnehaha, Laughing Water, the bride of Hiawatha, watched over by the dark shapes of menhirs on the hilltops.

I awoke to the croaking of a raven overhead somewhere, dreaming a nonsense of what E. M. Forster in *Howards End* called 'Borrow, Thoreau and sorrow', and squirmed half out of the sleeping bag like a caddis larva, watched by a curious, timid ewe and her lamb. There was a ruined roofless building by the bank of the waterfall pool and a rounded containing wall with a gate. I realised that this

must have been a sheep wash. It would explain the presence of the solitary sycamore providing shade over the
lawn where I was encamped, and a gnarled holly overhang-
ing the river as a sign for the shepherds. It might also be
the reason why this was the only place I had found daisies
and buttercups in the Rhinogs. They belong in the lowland
grazing meadows and would have been carried up here as
seeds or roots by sheep.

I leapt straight into the pool like a self-dipping sheep. It
was six feet deep, and I swam up to the waterfall and hung
there again in the bracing stream like a seagull following a
boat. Then I waded a little way downstream through the
disordered, foaming boulders to the next pool, in a gorge
of gleaming, mossy rock crossed by a bridge of six-foot
stone slabs slung across the water like the lintels of Stone-
henge. It was the wildest natural jacuzzi. Currents jostled
me from all directions and I climbed out stunned and gal-
vanised. I made tea on the gas stove and breakfasted on
more goats' cheese and bread. Although not quite up to the
standards of George Borrow, who sometimes breakfasted
on eggs, mutton chops, boiled and pickled salmon, fried
trout and potted shrimps, it was made special by the place,
with its buttercup lawn shaped into an inverted comma
and enclosed by a stone wall that retains the ancient, sloping track running past at a higher level, and tapers from
five feet to nothing in a way that a modern architect would
completely approve. There were surely never any drawings
for this, yet the proportions and sense of harmony with the

natural architecture of the water, rocks and trees were very fine. Whoever built it had, as Alexander Pope put it, 'consulted the genius of the place'. It was highly distinctive, like a Greek stage, shaped by years of use and now all the more beautiful for being a ruin and so remote. I had not seen a human soul for thirty-six hours, just sheep and the powerful presence of the Rhinogs, whose peaks that morning were lost in clouds. I could have stayed there for days, walking to the next tarn on the map with an unpronounceable name, and unpronounceably freezing water.

I could have stayed there for days, walking to the next tarn on the map with an unpronounceable name, and unpronounceably freezing water

6

Salmon-runs

DARTMOOR LOOKED DAUNTING, especially on the enormous map, which had taken up the whole of my billiard-table desk in the Map Room in Cambridge. Even on paper, I kept losing my place, running my finger along rivers spawned amidst the thin brown contours of peat-bogs, hills and tors. By the time I actually crossed the moor in the car the following afternoon, I was in a suitably wild, dark mood after sweating in traffic for hours on the way down through Somerset. It was one of several moments when I began seriously to question the whole outlandish project. I had naively imagined bouncing along the lanes of England in some open-topped bus, bursting with friends, their towels and costumes hung out to dry like flags in the breeze, and me at the wheel like Cliff Richard in *Summer Holiday*. Instead, of course, they were all far too busy with their own lives, and my journey was proving a much more solitary, even fugitive affair.

A cold dip in the West Dart River by the stone saddle bridge at Hexworthy came along just in time. I threw myself into a deep pool just upstream, gasping at the shock, and swam down into the stony salmon-haunts below. Surfacing, my spirits began to revive. I was, after all, on my way to visit friends; a family of Dartmoor river-swimmers. The West Dart is spectacular just here, dropping fast over the moor, surging at giant granite slabs ten or twelve feet long. I climbed round into the rapids above the pool and shot down into the eddy in the shadow of the bridge, disturbing a dipper that flew a rock or two away. The water tasted cold and fresh. Watched by a group of Japanese tourists on the bridge, I wallowed, splashed and dived, washing away the journey, feeling a little like an inexpert otter in the zoo, then dried off on warm granite. Half an hour later, the salmon were leaping there.

On Thursday afternoon I went with my friends, under oath of secrecy, to a bathing place where the Dart is joined by an unusually cold moorland torrent. We will call it the Sherberton Stream. Almost from its source in two springs high up beneath the summit of a tor, the torrent rushes headlong downhill, shaded by dense woodland all the way. So the springwater emerges into the Dart as cool as it was underground. The Dart slid like a white glacier into a deep, black pool, through a steep valley of oak and holly woods.

My friend John and I, wearing masks, snorkels and

flippers, dropped straight into deep water off some rocks and swam against the current up into the pool. What we saw there astonished us both. About ten feet down in the clear water, dappled with sunlight, lay dozens of salmon, many of them well over two feet long. They turned and nosed off languidly upstream at our approach, disappearing into the clear green bubbling river, or amongst the shadows of underwater rocks. We followed them upriver, then lost them. Coming back downstream in long, effortless strokes, we were ambushed from the left by the sudden shock of the chilly upland waters of the Sherberton Stream issuing into the pool. The unusually cold water, rich in oxygen, was the special attraction of this place for the salmon. John, who has swum here for over thirty years, had never seen this many fish in the pool. He is a geologist, now in his sixties, and during the 1960s and early '70s, he had his own flourishing Dartmoor tin mine. He still occasionally pans the river for tin or gold, more for pleasure than profit.

Dartmoor has always been rich in minerals. Ashburton and Buckfastleigh once had the biggest tin-mining industry in the world. They were the centre of a huge international trade that stretched all the way to Amsterdam, Byzantium and the Nile, and there is plenty of evidence of it in the river. John showed me the riffles where the mineral stones, sometimes gold or tin, collect in a natural pan. We waded about, looking for obstructions to the flow, like a quartz seam crossing the bed, and searched for tin and gold below them, panning the gravel with saucered hands. The metals are heavier than the rest of the river sediments and sink naturally into these hollows. We found tin nuggets, especially heavy and black, shaped like discarded chewing gum, but no gold. We scooped up haematite, too, named after the blood these dark nuggets of iron-ore resemble. Later on, in a field near the river at his home, John showed me the panning machine he had built in his workshop, a wonderfully Heath-Robinson affair with a rotating perforated steel drum that runs off a belt-drive from his tractor.

John and his family have developed their own river-swimming technique, and each year, before his daughters grew up, John used to take them for a long-distance swim down the river to Totnes. I tried out the novel style nervously the following morning in a fast stretch of the river that runs through fields near their house. John taught me how to swim the rapids, even sliding over the most unlikely shallows, by keeping my head down in the water and breathing through the snorkel. This automatically tilts the rest of your body higher in the water. You wear a wetsuit for protection from bruises, as well as cold, and you look ahead through your mask for fast-approaching rocks, keeping at least one arm outstretched to fend off as necessary. You propel yourself mostly with the flippers.

Seeing a boulder approaching you at high speed, with the irresistible force of the river behind you, is terrifying at first. But by surrendering your body to the current, it is surprising how easily and naturally you are swept down, like the translucent leaves you see dancing underwater in the sunlight. The current urges you along the best course, but you must keep steerage way as you would in a canoe, by swimming faster than the river. You realise why the otter's tail is called its rudder. Your mask seems to magnify things by framing them; and the sounds of the river, and your own breathing, are amplified underwater. You see churned gravel glittering like tinsel, old bricks with their maker's name nearly smoothed out, bright green pebbles, dark rusty haematite, a drowned plastic bag pinioned to a tangle of sticks, water shrimps, bands of bright shining quartz, passing fragments of flimsy waterweed, little bull-heads dodging under stones, and now and again the shadow of a trout. I swept on through a series of long, narrow, natural pools, steep-sided granite tanks that barrelled the river into deafening violence, hurling me down their gullets over dark submerged forms glimpsed skidding away, on past the wrecks of jammed tree-roots into the sudden calm of a deep pool.

Making my way back along the bank in the wetsuit through a field of cattle, carrying my flippers, mask and snorkel, I met the farmer, who said he had fished the Dart for thirty years. He wore tweed, I wore rubber and stood dripping, but he seemed not to notice, or was polite enough not to say anything, and we chatted away by the bank about otters and salmon for some considerable time. Before the war, he said, a favourite evening pastime of the Buckfastleigh citizens was to gather beside their weir and watch the otters playing. He said it was a good year for salmon and otters; there were more of both than he had ever known. He saw otter pads and prints on the sand here night after night and, only a few days before, he had actually seen an otter bitch and a cub; a rare occurrence. The Dart used to be polluted by dieldrin from the sheep-dip chemicals washed out of the wool at a carpet factory in Ashburton. The drastic decline in otters which began in the 1950s and led to their virtual extinction over most of England and Wales is known to have been caused by this very chemical. To make matters worse, the detergent used to wash the wool began over-enriching the river with phosphate and froth, but at last the river seems to be recovering, and the otters with it.

With so much twenty-four-carat water everywhere, there's a tradition of wild swimming in all the towns and villages that fringe the moor. At Throwleigh and South Zeal, they have always bathed and learnt to swim in a remote natural pool in the valley of the Blackaton Brook, which runs between steep banks of gorse and heather from the Raybarrow Pool at the foot of Cawsand Hill. The tiny waterhole was already naturally dammed by boulders, but enterprising swimmers gradually enlarged it by building the rocks higher. I heard about it from Mrs Amy Harvey, then nearly ninety, who had lived on Dartmoor all her life, and swam in this bathing hole throughout her childhood during the 1920s. She had written me a moving letter full of vivid recollections of the place, which is still popular with the village children now.

At Peter Tavy they have their own village swimming hole in the Colley Brook: a secluded mill-pool to which the bathers have added stone steps and a life-belt. I also visited the charming village swimming pool at Chagford, fed by the River Teign, with an outdoor café. It is fringed with trees down one side and – the last thing you expect to see on the edge of Dartmoor – a vigorous hedge of bamboo. The pool is filled from the river by a fast-flowing mill-stream that flows alongside it. These days, the Health and Safety people make them put chlorine in the water, but Pam, who lives in the cottage opposite and is the keyholder, doesn't like to put too much in because it spoils the fresh taste and smell of the clear river water off the moor. Pam's eighty-seven-year-old father-in-law, who helped to dig and build the original pool in 1947, comes down every day in the season and makes tea.

Okehampton used to have a river-fed pool a hundred feet long which was owned by a syndicate of swimmers, but has since been filled in. People who grew up swimming here in the 'ice cold water' remember the strict pre-war caretaker, Mr Wallers. He would open the baths at seven o'clock on a Sunday morning so people could swim before going on to shiver in church or Sunday school. He then closed up for the rest of the day. This is what Dartmoor Puritanism is all about.

Rivers rise everywhere on the moor. In the peat beneath

Great Kneeset, five rivers have their beginnings: the Taw, Tavy, Teign, Torridge and Dart. But of all the Dartmoor rivers, the Erme is the most secretive. It rises in the long shadow of Hartor Tor and flows south through Ivybridge into a farm landscape around Holbeton so hilly that everyone gets an aerial view of their neighbour. Fields, barns and hedgerows are tilted at all angles like the counterpane of an unmade bed.

I had been curious about the Erme ever since first hearing Mike Westbrook's *The Cortège*, a large-scale work for jazz instruments and voices in which one movement, 'Erme Estuary', is a response to the place where he and Kate Westbrook live. It ends with a long, other-worldly solo on the electric guitar. But the estuary was all too real, and none too warm, as I swam across it on the rising tide two days later, seeing it for the first time on a visit to my musical friends. I had crossed to the centre of the wide bay from Coastguard's Beach. A little group of surfers clustered waist deep, waiting for the big grey rollers that surged out of the open sea, breaking on a sandbar. I threw myself in with them and swam inland. I felt the incoming tide lock on to my legs and thrust me in towards the distant woods along the shore. Each time a frond of sea-lettuce lightly brushed me, or glued itself around my arms, I thought it was a jellyfish, and flinched. But I soon grew used to it; seaweed was all around me, sliding down each new wave to drape itself about me. I kept on swimming until I practically dissolved, jostled from behind by the swell. Then, as the tide rose higher, the sandy estuary beach came into focus. The woods reached right over the water, and began accelerating past me. I found I was moving at exhilarating speed, in big striding strokes, like a fell runner on the downhill lap. It was like dream swimming, going so effortlessly fast, and feeling locked in by the current, with no obvious means of escape. I was borne along faster and faster as the rising tide approached the funnel of the river's mouth until it shot me into a muddy, steep-sided mooring channel by some old stone limekilns on the beach. I had to strike out with all my strength to escape the flood and reach the eddy in the shallows. I swam back up to the limekilns and crawled out on to the beach like a turtle, but couldn't resist dropping back into the muscular current for a second ride down the channel.

Earlier, we had all picnicked on Mothecombe Beach together, to the west of the estuary, and Mike and I had swum in the bay. It was a Private Day at the beach, which meant that only bona fide local villagers from Holbeton were allowed access, and then only to one side, leaving the other free for the private enjoyment of the Mildmay-White family, who own it. The whole of the lovely Erme estuary might have been rechristened the Baring Straits, since all the surrounding land was originally purchased in the 1870s by the two cousins who controlled Barings Bank: Edward Baring and Alfred Mildmay-White. Mothecombe is a private beach, and the estate charges the public for access via a man in a small wooden ticket-office at the top of the cliff path. The wild beauty of the coastal estate was evidence of sensitive management.

Mike had come round by the cliff path to our rendezvous at the limekilns, and we stood gazing across the estuary. A dense unbroken canopy of English rainforest flowed down to the water everywhere. It was an almost tropical scene, with six or seven egrets decoratively arranged in an oak, or flying with their long legs outstretched. I had seen them the previous summer on the Arne peninsula in Dorset, where they have even begun to nest. They are now a regular feature of the south coast of England, no longer confined to Spain, Portugal and North Africa. As the tide advanced, we stood listening to the sucking of millions of tiny worms in their mudholes. On the far shore there stood a single boat-house, reflected in the mud, half-hidden in the woods.

As I changed on the beach, we witnessed a scene like a cameo from fifty years ago. A mother, grandmother and a little boy caught crabs in a net baited with chicken from under a rock the grandmother had known as a secret crabbing place from her own childhood. What I found so inspiring about this vignette was the element of continuity that it shared with Mrs Harvey's story of the Blackaton Brook bathing hole. Two generations later, the crabs were still under their rock, and the village children were still swimming in the wild pool.

On the way home, we passed a reed-bed alive with the free improvisation of a sedge warbler ensemble, performing solos like earthy, uninhibited saxophones. Westbrook clearly felt at home with them, quoting the birdbook description of their 'irresponsible song' with approval. We stood on a wooden bridge watching a procession of seaweed carried up by the tide. It created the curious illusion that we and the bridge were moving like a boat through the water, back out to sea.

7

Extinctions

NEXT DAY I met an otter in the Waveney. I swam round a bend in my favourite river in Suffolk and there it was, sunning itself on a floating log near the reed-bed. I would have valued a moment face to face, but it was too quick for that. It slipped into the water on the instant, the big paddle tail following through with such stealth that it left hardly a ripple. But I saw its white bib and the unmistakable bulk of the animal, and I knew I had intruded into its territory; knew also that it was underwater somewhere close, sensing my movements. It hadn't paused to puzzle over my unconventional mode of approach. It just went. It didn't miss a beat. We can scarcely be said to have communed, yet I can replay every frame of the brief encounter in slow motion, right down to the just-vacated wet log rolling back into balance, oscillating slightly, and my own emotions, a mixture of elation at a rare moment's audience with the most reclusive animal on the river (Ted Hughes called it 'a king in hiding') and shame at having interrupted its private reverie.

That otters came within a whisker of extinction in England and Wales during the late fifties and early sixties is well known. It happened suddenly and insidiously. But there are hopeful signs that they are now gradually returning to many of their traditional rivers. It has taken thirty years for the powerful poisons that killed them, organochloride pesticides like aldrin, dieldrin and DDT, to flush out of our rivers, and for people to realise that otters will only thrive in waters that are left wild and untutored, as well as unpolluted, with plenty of wet woodland, untidy wood stacks, nettles, story-book gnarled trees full of hollows, and as few humans as possible.

I was swimming ten miles from the moat, where the Waveney defines the border between Norfolk and Suffolk. It is a secret river, by turns lazy and agile, dashing over shallow beds of golden gravel, then suddenly quiet, dignified and deep. It winds through water meadows, damp woods and marshes in a wide basin that was once tidal from Yarmouth to Diss, close to its source in the great watershed of Redgrave Fen, where its twin, the Little Ouse, also rises and flows off in the opposite direction, into the Fens. With its secret pools and occasional sandy beaches, the Waveney is full of swimming holes, diving stages improvised from wooden pallets, dangling ropes, and upturned canoes pulled up on the bank. Every two or three miles you come to a weir and a whitewashed watermill.

I swam on beyond the otter pool, under some sort of spell. It struck me that the animal's particular magic does not stem so much from its rarity as its invisibility. It is through their puckish, Dionysian habit of veiling themselves from view that otters come to embody the river spirits themselves. Henry Williamson knew this when he wrote his great mythic poem of Tarka the Otter. In the best traditions of spirits, the otter reveals itself through signs. You hunt for their tracks on sandbars, or for their spraint, the aromatic dung they leave behind to mark their territory, like clues in an Easter-egg hunt, under bridges or on the lowest boughs of willow or alder.

That otters were once plentiful in the Waveney was clear enough until recently if you went to the Harleston Magpie, which used to be a principal meeting place for the Eastern Counties Otter Hounds. Before the pub was altered, there were still otter masks and pads on the walls there, and up the road at the De la Pole Arms in Wingfield they have even installed entire animals, mummified in glass cases. One of my Suffolk friends inherited a red and blue tweed hunting coat that would have been worn by a member of the Eastern Counties Otter Hounds. It must have been hot work, hurrying on foot up and down the river bank, and from pub to pub along the valley, in tweed suits. A student of rural customs, he also once saw an otter pad mounted on a wooden shield with the enigmatic inscription: 'Shanghai Otter Hounds, Wortwell Mill, 1912'. Quite by chance, he stumbled on the explanation in a bookshop the following year, looking through the memoirs of an officer of the Shanghai Police, Maurice Springfield, who, it seemed, had been the Master of the Shanghai Otter Hounds, and bought some of the dogs in Suffolk around 1912 to take back with him to China. He must have been allowed to hunt them with the East Anglian contingent, perhaps by way of a road test, running down the unfortunate otter at Wortwell Mill.

In the autumn of the year before, I had crossed Suffolk to Westleton Village Hall one Saturday morning to attend a training session in animal tracking organised by the Suffolk Wildlife Trust so that we could take part in a survey of the Suffolk rivers for otters, mink and water voles. About forty of us sat in the hall studying slides of their footprints, and learning more about their ways. Small plastic tubs containing otter and mink shit were solemnly passed round. It was a bit like a wine tasting. You waved the poos under your nose, sniffed, then passed on the sample to your neighbour. Our tutor described otter spraint as 'fragrant', with something of the quality of jasmine tea, but perhaps an added nuance of fish oil and new-mown hay. A sample of jasmine tea was also circulated. You need a good nose to be a successful otter detective. We took it on trust from our tutor that otter spraint is also 'tarry and tacky'. Mink, on the other hand, have, or do, 'scats'. Scats look quite like spraint, but smell like burnt rubber or rotten fish. I felt the aesthetics of the matter posed some threat to our scientific objectivity.

That afternoon, we had all gone down to the Eel's Foot at Eastbridge, within sight of the Sizewell B nuclear power station, and walked along the bank of the Minsmere river in a crocodile looking for real live otter spraint. The Minsmere otters, no doubt observing all this from the safety of some hollow tree, would have witnessed the unusual spectacle of forty humans queuing to lie full-length on the bank and sniff small dollops of poo, making appreciative sounds. Someone spotted a bubble and all forty of us froze, bright-eyed and bushy-tailed, but it was just a bubble. I find I have since rather gone off jasmine tea.

THE FOLLOWING AFTERNOON, I swam the length of Benacre Broad at Covehithe a few miles up the coast the other side of Southwold. It is a silty fresh-water lagoon separated from the sea by a low spit of sand and shingle beach, and its days are numbered. The bleached skeleton of a single tree stood defiantly in the middle of the sands. As I swam back in water like cooled tea towards the spit, and the sea beyond, rooks cawed in the dark woods behind me, and a curlew called from the reed-beds. Long Covert, the old bluebell wood beside the broad, is blindly marching into the sea. In spring, bluebells and pink campions grow right up to the pebble strand, which is strewn with the decaying roots and stumps of oaks and sycamores. Meanwhile, the sea was pickling the trees at the edge of the wood to extinction. First it shrivelled their leaves, then it blasted them until the trunks were white and bare. I stepped thirty paces over the beach and swam out into the North Sea.

I had come down the path along the disintegrating cliffs from the magnificent ruined church at Covehithe. Each year, the path moves further inland across the fields because great hunks of England keep falling away in the winter storms. The previous year Roger Middleditch, the beleaguered farmer, had planted carrots. By the time he came to harvest them, they were sticking out of the cliff-top and littering the beach like fish. A year later, his rows of lemming barley grew right up to the cliff and toppled over it. During the winter, Mr Middleditch had lost about twelve metres to the sea. Two years before, he had lost twenty. Since the mid-1970s, when the erosion mysteriously began to accelerate, the waves have taken forty-seven acres of the farm. It was originally nearly 300 acres; now it is 240. Less than four acres of a twenty-one-acre field that led the other way to the sea from the farm in the 1970s now remain. His philosophical words came back to me as I drove away down the lanes towards Dunwich: 'In less than twenty-five years the sea will have reached the church and our farm. The church will go, the farmhouse and buildings will go, Benacre Broad will disappear.'

Richard Mabey, who has often walked the East Anglian beaches, has a sense of the way this shifting coastline may work on the mind: 'I sometimes wondered if the closeness of these unstable edges of the land was part of the secret of Norfolk's appeal to us, a reflection of a half-conscious desire to be as contingent as spindrift ourselves, to stay loose, cast off, be washed up somewhere unexpected.'

THAT EVENING, I visited Suffolk's own lost city of Atlantis, and swam at nightfall over the drowned churches of Dunwich. Pilgrims have been coming here for years to gaze at what no longer is, or to look out to sea in rough weather and listen for the fabled submarine ringing of the bells of fifty sunken churches; perhaps even to pen a line or two like: 'Where frowns the ruin o'er the silent dead.' The tide was almost up, and I swam off the steep bank of shingle by the fishermen's huts. The clattering pebbles, dragged by the swell like castanets, were amplified by the night, and by the cool evening water. The moon was strung on the horizontal vapour trail of a jet plane like a musical note printed on a page.

There never were anything like fifty churches, although a Southwold historian, Thomas Gardner, had said so in 1754 and the exaggeration stuck, along with the underwater pealing of church bells, supposedly swung by the same rampaging sea that had demolished the medieval city and port on the night of 14 January 1328. Hundreds of homes, barns and warehouses in six parishes were eventually inundated. By 1573, only two churches were left standing, and most of what remained except for All Saints' church was destroyed in the great storm of 1740. But one of the church towers still stood perfectly upright on the beach at low tide, until it collapsed in about 1900. So thorough has been the sea's erasure that almost the only historical evidence left is in documentary records. The tempest didn't just take churches, shops and houses, it took hills, a whole hunting forest, and the major harbour on which the city's prosperity was founded. It washed them all away like a sandcastle and blocked the entrance to the harbour with a gigantic shingle bank, closing it forever. The contrast between the clamour of a medieval sea-port city at the peak of prosperity and the empty, silent horizon of today is enough to set the least reflective of souls thinking about the impermanence of things. All that is left of Dunwich now (apart from the car park) is a café, a pub, two fishermen's huts, a row of houses, and a nineteenth-century church. The one medieval building still standing is the ruined twelfth-century chapel of the St James leper hospital, once well outside the city walls. There is something of the myth of Philoctetes about its survival: the outsiders have endured in the end.

The uncomfortable pebble beach shelves steeply, and I was glad to subside into the sea, swimming immediately in deep water, black and treacly after the lightness of the Waveney the day before. Far out past the breakers, shifting like a porpoise in the swell, I had the illusion that the shadowy cliffs were visibly receding. The underlying boulder clay of Suffolk erodes easily, and the layer of shingle that lies on top of it is forever being washed away and moved about by storms and tides to create an undersea topography that changes so much, they have to keep redrawing the navigation charts. I was the only bather in the cool night sea, and everything was very distant. To the north, the lighthouse at Southwold; towards the horizon, a cargo ship and a fishing boat, and to the south at Sizewell, the brash twinkling of the nuclear power station. Moving through the night, suspended in the waves over the extinct city, was like swimming over the submerged Iron Age fields of the Scilly Isles.

8

An Encounter with Naiads

Yorkshire Dales, 13 August

THERE IS A LONG tradition of wild swimming in Yorkshire. Sweating out a shift in the heat and dust underground, coal miners must have cast their thoughts longingly, in summer, towards the abundant cooling rivers and becks of the limestone country of the Dales. In no other industry was communal, ritual bathing such a deeply essential part of life; there were always showers or baths at the head of the pit. Getting into water is still second nature in this part of the world. Hill walking and cycling have always been popular in the north, and the Dales are full of tempting swimming holes to cool one's weary frame. The springs and underground streams burst everywhere from the labyrinthine limestone. Every village has its favourite places, some of them secret and difficult to reach, and often actually called this or that 'hole', like Foss

Hole and Chemist Hole, in the superb River Doe above Ingleton.

The Yorkshire Dales have been shaped and carved by rivers. The Swale, Ure, Nidd, Wharfe, Ribble, Aire, Skirfare and Tees all rise in these hills, with the Lune running south to Lancaster out of Cumbria, and the Eden running north to Carlisle. With such abundance of water, few places are richer in wild flowers than limestone country, and Richard Mabey, an aficionado of the Dales, had intrigued me with a chance remark that set me off on a quest for a particularly remote and enchanting swimming hole above Littondale. His caution that I would probably have to abseil down to it only increased my curiosity. He described a clear tufa pool hidden in a cleft somewhere up a beck, guarded by a limestone canyon on the walk between Arncliffe and Malham. This was too interesting not to pursue, and in any case I couldn't get the place-names he mentioned out of my head: Cowside Beck and Yew Cogar Scar.

At the Falcon Hotel on the village green in Arncliffe, I was awoken early by the screaming of swifts, and a swallow singing in the eves over my open sash-window. It reminded me of home. The little hotel is a haunt of trout anglers on the River Skirfare, a tributary of the Wharfe, and nothing much seemed to have changed since 1950. It was just the sort of place I could imagine T. H. White holing up in for the weekend.

I set out across country towards Malham, climbing up along the top of the steep-sided gorge that contained the beck. The tiny figure of a cyclist laboured up the road on the other side towards Settle – 'a cruel road', they called it in the pub. Everything here carried the signs of use: the path, the sheep-holes worn brown into the hillside, the polished pine handholds of the stile ladders. Massive stone walls plunged almost vertically down the steep sides of the dale to the beck in perfectly straight lines, and the limestone strata showed through the grass like flock in a threadbare sofa.

The sun had come out, and glinted in the Cowside Beck, clearly audible three or four hundred feet below. About two miles further on up the high ridge path I came to a declivity diving towards the increasingly distant bottom of the gorge. There was no path, and the descent was so precipitous that it was impossible to see more than a few yards ahead at a time, but I decided to take the plunge, more or less literally, towards the beck. It was hard to know, even with the help of the map, whether I was heading down towards Yew Cogar Scar, the spectacular cliffs that walled parts of the gorge. They live up to their name with a perpendicular forest of gnarled yews that somehow clings to the rock face. The escarpment I hoped I was going down was Cowside. The descent was so dizzy it was hardly even grazed, so there were tussocks full of ankle-sized potholes. A stiff breeze funnelled up the gorge threatening to shake off the gaudy yellow-and-black-striped humbug snails that clung to harebells and yellow bedstraw. I felt for them, hanging on for dear life too, and creeping blindly down. The really amazing thing was that there were trees. Bent old rowan, ash and hawthorn grew from the most daring rocky outcrops, probably the only places where a sapling would have escaped being grazed. Fortunately, I had brought a climbing rope which I looped round a trunk wherever I could, and so slithered my way in stages to the bottom.

By now I was feeling the thrill of the chase, glancing eagerly about in search of hidden pools. I had landed in the canyon bottom just upstream from the cliffs of yew. The first thing I saw was a black rabbit disappearing into a stone wall, then another. Was there a whole colony of them marooned in here? Looking up at the imposing rocks, I could have been in California. I had no idea how I was going to climb out again. I followed the beck upstream, rounding each bend and contour with the warm glow of anticipated pleasure.

At length I came upon a small spinney of ash by the banks, and the promising sound of a waterfall. And there, just below, was the elusive tufa pool and the sparkle of animated water chasing its tail around in it. It was very nearly circular, and rimmed with moss. At one side, natural steps led into its perfectly clear depths, which ran to eight or ten feet by the fall. I stripped and dived in. It was so cold, I might have flung myself into a bed of nettles. Then came the heady rush of the endorphins, or 'endolphins' as a friend once called them, the natural opiates with which the body anaesthetises itself against the cold, and the adrenaline. As the *Oxford Textbook of Medicine* cautiously says, the mood changes they induce 'are difficult to validate scientifically, although feelings of well-being seem to occur'. For swimmers, my friend's inspired malapropism goes straight to the point: you come up feeling like a dolphin. The Cowside Beck dashed towards me like a wind under the trees, and spouted smoothly between two rocks to hurtle into the pool, which I now explored, feeling beneath the bubbling surface with hands and feet, diving under, and swimming against the current to hover in the middle. Immediately uphill, a tributary stream cascaded down a series of waterfalls and saucered pools over mounds of tufa accumulated through the centuries. If it weren't so natural and ancient, it would be easy to mistake tufa for the kind of artificial rocks you see at the Chelsea Flower Show. It is really petrified water that has built up, like the fur in a kettle, from the lime that is carried in the streams. It is voluptuous and spongy and loves to dress itself in fine mosses and algae.

I flopped out on to a rock, up the grassy side, and clambered, dripping, to bathe in a second pool some thirty yards upstream. The boisterous water took my breath away all over again and I returned to the circular pool, where I swam down once more to the bottom under the waterfall and surfaced inside it, coming out with head, hands and feet frozen, feeling wonderful. I thawed them in the gentle, dished, tufa pool, like a warm bath after the frigid beck, its water slipping over the sunlit stone.

I wondered how many walkers must have slid into these tempting waters, remote and hidden though they are. Sunlight reflected back off the rounded white rocks on the bottom, and soft cushions of fine, tight grass and thyme were scattered languidly around the margin, as though for some nocturnal gathering of the nymphs. J. B. Priestley, when he was travelling about these parts in 1933, met a woman who lived in one of the remote Dales farmhouses, 'a solid West Riding countrywoman and not one of your fanciful arts-and-crafts misses', who swore that she saw faeries dancing on the hillside. There are still some places left in England that have unquestioned magic about them. This pool had me enchanted; I could have stayed there quite happily all day and night with the attendant naiads. But a man must take care never to kiss a water sprite. As the English folk-song 'George Collins' relates, it will lead to certain death, and that of any woman he subsequently kisses. The old pagan deities may have fled much of our land, but they have not yet forsaken all their haunts.

Made ravenous by the cold water, I demolished a prosaic sandwich lunch reclining on a cushion of thyme, with my head resting on a clump of moss the size and texture of a British Railways antimacassar, then decided to climb up alongside the tributary gill, through a scree of scattered rock, past the occasional modest waterfall, towards some caves at the top of Cowside. Sleepy dor-beetles crept about in the grass, and Yorkshire rabbits darted out everywhere, more agile than their lazy Suffolk cousins, bouncing between the rocks like bagatelle balls. The head of the steep cleft was a mass of springs spouting extravagantly over a giant sponge of tufa, decked out in mosses, ferns, liverworts and algae. I sat in the cave and ate another cheese sandwich, spiced with sorrel leaves I had gathered on the way up, grateful for the generous hint that sent me to this wild and beautiful spa.

9

A Descent into Hell Gill

Yorkshire/Cumbria border, 18 August

BACK IN BERNIE'S CAFÉ at Ingleton, they had told me to expect an experience somewhere between potholing, swimming, surfing and rock-climbing if I ever ventured down the inside of Hell Gill. To find it, I was going to have to trek over the wild moorland of Abbotside Common beyond Wensleydale and Garsdale Head. After an indolent morning in the wilds of Barbondale, I drove up through Garsdale, took the road towards Kirkby Stephen, and parked the car half in Yorkshire, half in Cumbria, astride the county boundary. To walk up the Hell Gill beck on a sunny afternoon out of the vale of the River Eden (of which it is the headwater) was my idea of heaven. There were foxgloves and trout, and a buzzard sailing lazily aloft. From here, the Eden runs north through Appleby to Carlisle, and something odd must have happened in the upheaval of the Ice Age, because Hell Gill is only yards away from the source of the River Ure, which flows the opposite way, to the Humber.

I had packed a rope and wetsuit boots in the rucksack and followed a track over the Settle to Carlisle railway line and uphill past Hell Gill Farm, following the beck to a bridge and a small wood that grows around the precipitous gorge that brought me here. I skirted past it uphill, and there, suddenly, was the entrance to the canyon. The beck just funnelled between four rocks and disappeared into the hillside in a steep, concealed cleft. Even from a few yards away, you wouldn't know it was there, and the hidden character of the beck is one possible origin of its name, from the old Teutonic *Hala*, 'the coverer up, or hider', and the verb *hel*, to hide. Looking down into the chasm, listening to the wild clamour of the hissing water pressing forward over the brink, I felt like a child at the top of the helter-skelter, or some equally dubious fairground ride: not at all sure this was such a good idea.

The Hell Gill gorge is like a pothole whose roof has cracked open sixty feet or more above. It plunges almost vertically down the hillside for four hundred yards in a continuous series of waterfalls dropping into overflowing pools of hollowed limestone. Geologically, the tunnelling of the limestone probably began at the end of the last Ice Age, 11,000 years ago, when the melt-water from above, finding no other way out, flowed down through alternate strata of limestone, shale and sandstone higher up the hill, and, still trapped by the glacier overhead, burst down a weakness in the limestone layer it encountered here, and bored out the gorge by dissolving the rock.

My temporary state of funk took the form of an impromptu exploration of the upstream beck in the afternoon sun. It forms the county boundary here, and with all the energy of the serious procrastinator, I waded and swam my way upstream, criss-crossing from Yorkshire to Cumbria between huge slabs of grey limestone crammed with fossils. Trout lay in the riffles and darted into shadows. I wallowed in a five-foot-deep waterfall pool, and found vast water-slides, twenty- and thirty-foot tablets of the smoothed limestone that was once coral reefs rising out of a tropical seabed 280 million years ago. Here you could bathe all day without meeting a soul, and better still, know in your heart that you would be undisturbed. A hawk had been killing pigeons, butchering them on the rock beside the water here and there. The black stains on the limestone, and stuck feathers, accentuated the desolation of the moor.

Courage up, I returned to the turbulent rim of the gorge and did what I knew might be an unwise thing. I couldn't help it. I began to slide into the mouth of the abyss itself. I found myself in the first of a series of smooth limestone cups four or five feet in diameter and anything between three and five feet deep, stepped at an acute angle down a flooded gulley of hollowed limestone that spiralled into the unknown. In the low light, the smooth, wet walls were a beautiful aquamarine, their shining surface intricately pock-marked like the surface of the moon. All my instincts were to hold on, but to what? The ice and the water had polished everything perfectly. The torrent continually sought to sweep me with it, and so I slithered and climbed down Hell Gill's dim, glistening insides, through a succession of cold baths, in one long primal scream.

There is something atavistic about all swimming, but this was so intensely primitive it was visceral. I felt like Jonah inside the whale. Each time I dropped, or was swept, into a new cauldron, I thought it would be bottomless; the turbulence made the water opaque. Borne down this magical uterus, deafened by the rushing and boiling of the flood, with the sheer rock and just a crack of sky high above me, I felt at once apprehensive and exhilarated. Water was cupped, jugged, saucered, spooned, decanted, stirred and boiled. It was thrown up in a fine spray so you breathed it in, it splashed in your face, it got in your ears, it stung you with its force, it bounced back off every curving surface, it worked unremittingly to sculpt the yielding limestone into the forms of its own well-ordered movement. Beneath the apparent chaos, all this sound and fury conformed to the strict laws of fluid dynamics.

So steep and labyrinthine was the descent that it was impossible to know or see what was to come next. The slippery blue-green wetness and smoothness of everything, and my near-nakedness, only made me more helpless, more like a baby. It was like a dream of being born. Unnamed thunderings like deep, booming heartbeats rose from somewhere below. It was exactly as Frederick Leboyer said in *Birth Without Violence*: 'The horror of being born is the intensity, the immensity of the experience, its variety, its suffocating richness . . . It is a sensory experience so huge, it is beyond our comprehension.'

Everyone I had talked to about this descent had said that once you're in, you must keep on going down, because you can't climb up. I was glad of the rubber boots and the grip of their soles, but the rope was no use at all because every surface was so perfectly smoothed there was nothing to loop it round. I was conscious that I shouldn't really be doing this alone. I had impetuously broken the first rule of potholing or climbing: that you let somebody know where you're heading before you set out. The feeling became acute as I reached a waterfall that sounded as if it dropped to Australia, and might be the source of the thundering Pink Floyd 'Atom Heart Mother' effects. They were becoming louder and more insistent.

Suddenly I found myself beneath an overhang of rock. A rope was bolted in here and there, and stretched off into a gloomy void beyond. It was impossible to see where it led, how deep the pool below might be, or how far down. I had no idea where the next foothold was. The torrent just shot over a rocky lip and disappeared from view, into a gothic emptiness. One option was to plunge blindly towards the waterfall and hope to drop into the pool, which might be deep enough for a safe landing. But the voices of reason shouted above the din that I stood an equal chance of being dashed into a rock face. The dilemma, and the stark solitude of my predicament, set my mind racing feverishly. I considered that for all I knew I might find myself, like the climber in H. G. Wells's story 'The Country of the Blind', marooned in a subterranean land full of people like myself who had strayed optimistically down the Hell Gill chasm and stranded themselves beyond the waterfall. I also recalled that in the story, the sightless majority propose to put out the eyes of the newcomer.

I pondered my position carefully, still thinking fast because every minute I spent immobile I was getting wetter and colder. Normally, you would clip on to an overhead rope, but I had no harness. I had met a pair of potholers down by the road and spoken to them briefly. They were accoutred in harnesses, buckles and steel clips like door-to-door ironmongers, and I now cursed my failure to ask them about Hell Gill. Once over the edge and dangling from the rope there was no going back. I would have to go hand over hand down it with fingers that were by now half-numb. But how far? I didn't fancy being stuck in a freezing beck all night in swimming trunks. On the other hand I had been told it was impossible to climb back up. Was it really? I wondered. I spent what seemed an eternity fighting my reluctance to turn back and accepting a growing conviction of the logic of at least attempting the ascent. The slight fading of the afternoon light filtering down led me to my decision. I would try going up through the cascading water, and, if I failed, then I would just have to risk going down instead. With the help of strung nerves, the rubber boots, and liberal helpings of adrenalin, I managed to heave myself up the narrow chimney from pool to pool, waterfall to waterfall, against the water. It was slow going, making my way up like a salmon, and I resolved to return some day with a companion, a little more local knowledge, and the right kit.

Emerging at last at the mouth of the gorge, I glanced back at it with faint disbelief and greeted the sky. Then, having dressed, I wandered a little way up the beck in the warm evening and fell asleep on the grass like a new-born babe. I was woken with a jolt by the searing rush of a buzzard stooping on an unwary pigeon. There was a silent explosion of pale grey feathers, like a distant shell. I felt a breath of wind in the grass that could have been a white rabbit hurrying by. 'I've had such a curious dream!' I said to myself, and went off for my tea.

10

The Walberswick Shiverers

Suffolk, 25 December

I HAD INVITED a group of friends to come and celebrate my journey's end with a Christmas Day swim in the North Sea. There was little enough good cheer about the weather when we arrived in Walberswick: driving rain and breakers the colour of dirty knickers licking up the beach. We had arranged to meet at eleven o'clock at the Hidden Hut, a clapboard and pebble-dash seaside bungalow with a surprisingly enormous sitting room warmed by a woozing wood stove. My friends Lucy and Madeleine had rented it for the week, and the sweet smell of onion soup already simmering on the hob greeted me as I stepped in out of the horizontal rain to join the gently steaming group in front of the stove. Amongst them were Tim and Meg, serious year-round bathers with a beach hut at Southwold, in a sedate row named after the English monarchs. Theirs is called 'Karl'. Tim broke the news to me that for the first time in years he was going to have to forgo his Christmas North Sea dip because of a touch of flu. Everyone else, however, already had their swimming costumes on under their clothes, ready for a quick change by the sea.

Apart from Tim and Meg, none of us was in the habit of doing this sort of thing, but I had the idea of starting something in Walberswick along the lines of the original Hove Shiverers, who began life in the early 1920s with a handful of winter swimmers, and still meet on Christmas Day. I had been stirred to action by reading one of their early annual reports, written in February 1931, which included the ringing words:

> Ten years ago there were no Shiverers. Ten years ago serious winter swimming was at a standstill in our district, and the Hove baths closed its hospitable doors in the winter evenings. People who worked all day, or children who went to school, if they wished to swim in the evening had no choice but the sea. A few swimmers, newcomers to Hove, looked at the prospect one winter's night and shivered, and that shiver has spread until nearly a thousand now join in the vibration.

With a last glance at the smug little wood stove, we set off for the beach in the slanting, stinging rain driven by a freak wind from the south-west. It was cold, yet there was a hint of mercy in this wind and it lacked the bite of the usual winter draughts that come straight from Russia to bear-hug the Walberswick dunes.

When we arrived on the beach and confronted the sea, the entire swimming party spontaneously bottled out. This was outright mutiny, a wholesale desertion by the Walberswick Shiverers, but what could I do? I was left gamely trying to balance on one leg in the wind and struggle out of a pair of long-johns and into my frozen Speedos. Trunks always seem especially sensitive to the relative humidity of the surrounding atmosphere. Like the seaweed we used to bring home from holiday to hang up by the back door and forecast the weather, costumes breathe in humidity and hold on to it. They never quite dry out, even dangling before the fire all night. The long-johns got stuck round my ankles, and wrestled me on to the wet pebbles just as more well-insulated well-wishers, Virginia and Florence, came into sight along the beach, Virginia in a massive fake ocelot coat, me in goosepimples.

Once in the trunks, I wasted no time getting rainswept, and strode with as much casual determination as I could muster straight into the khaki waves. The sea was not quite as cold as I had feared when I woke up in the night and thought about it, but it was still a case of gritting my teeth and thinking of England for that first moment or two. Having the loyal Shiverers on the beach was a big boost to the morale or, put another way, a big deterrent to copping out. I would, however, have preferred them to be in the water with me. Once fully immersed and striking out for deeper water, I experienced the intoxication of the fiery cold, and found myself splashing about and even body-surfing with manic energy. A dog spotted me and thought it would come and join in the fun. It scampered down to the shore, got one paw wet and instantly retreated. I stayed in far longer than I had intended and even received a modest round of applause when I emerged, to the outstretched towels and concerned piling-on of warm sweaters normally reserved for young children. Very welcome it was too, and my knees glowed bright purple as our party of non-playing swimmers crunched back, still snug in their bathing costumes, towards the beach huts and over the dunes, home to the Hidden Hut and Lucy's onion soup.

ROGER DEAKIN was a writer, filmmaker, traveller and conservation-ist. During his varied career he worked as an advertising copywriter and an English teacher, was a founding member of Friends of the Earth and a co-founder of the environmental group Common Ground. In 1969 Deakin bought Walnut Tree Farm, a moated Elizabethan farmhouse in Suffolk, where he lived for 38 years, swimming almost daily in the moat.

Deakin's book *Waterlog*, published in 1999 and from which this Mini is extracted, brought him international fame and the affection of readers and swimmers everywhere. The book broke new ground in calling for the right to swim in wild and open water, and as a work of nature writing it remains a classic of its genre. The launch party for the book was held at the Oasis open-air swimming pool in central London.

RECOMMENDED BOOKS BY ROGER DEAKIN:

Waterlog
Wildwood
Notes from Walnut Tree Farm

Enjoy Swimming?

Eating
NIGELLA LAWSON

VINTAGE MINIS

Liberty
VIRGINIA WOOLF

VINTAGE MINIS

Summer
LAURIE LEE

VINTAGE MINIS

Desire
HARUKI MURAKAMI

VINTAGE MINIS

VINTAGE MINIS

The Vintage Minis bring you the world's greatest writers on the experiences that make us human. These stylish, entertaining little books explore the whole spectrum of life – from birth to death, and everything in between. Which means there's something here for everyone, whatever your story.

vintageminis.co.uk